OTTAWA

THE UNKNOWN CITY

OTTAWA
THE UNKNOWN CITY

rob mclennan

ARSENAL
PULP PRESS

VANCOUVER

ARSENAL PULP PRESS
200 – 341 Water Street
Vancouver, BC
Canada V6B 1B8
arsenalpulp.com

The publisher gratefully acknowledges the support of the Government of Canada through the
Book Publishing Industry Development Program and the Government of British Columbia through
the Book Publishing Tax Credit Program for its publishing activities.

Efforts have been made to locate copyright holders of source material wherever possible. The
publisher welcomes hearing from any copyright holders of material used in this book who have
not been contacted.

Text and cover design by Electra Design Group
Cover photography by Tony Tremblay
Edited by Derek Fairbridge
Edited for the press by Bethanne Grabham

Printed and bound in Canada

Library and Archives Canada Cataloguing in Publication:

McLennan, Rob, 1970-
        Ottawa : the unknown city / Rob McLennan.

(Unknown city)

Includes bibliographical references and index.
ISBN 978-1-55152-232-6

        1. Ottawa (Ont.)–Guidebooks. I. Title. II. Series.

FC3096.18.M34 2008   917.13'84045   C2007-904434-4

c o n t e n t s

This book is for my mother, Joanne Irene Page McLennan

acknowledgments

Thanks, whether for information or conversation, to various friends and sources, including "American John" Alexander, Jonathan Browns, Alida Cupillari, Amanda Earl, Emily Falvey, Jenn Farr, Adrian Göllner, Anita Lahey, Marcus McCann, Janet McGowan at the National Capital Commission, Arthur McGregor, James Moran, Jennifer Mulligan, Monty Reid, Wendy Thomson, Evan Thornton, and Steve Zytveld; Kathy Watchum at Jack Purcell Community Centre; Shayna Keces and Brian Silcoff in the Ottawa Room of the Ottawa Public Library; Charles Earl and John W. MacDonald for their magnificent photographs; and everyone at Arsenal Pulp Press: Brian, Shyla, Robert, and Bethanne for their assistance and their patience.

introduction

In Ottawa, change has been the only constant. The city has gone through countless transformations over the years, from the time of the Algonquin and Outaouais First Nations peoples, to the end of New France in 1759 and subsequent British rule that brought American immigrants, including a group led by lumber baron Philemon Wright, who settled across the river in Hull Township. From the day when Ottawa was named capital of this young country, to today when Ottawa is a still-growing, bustling government town – the city continues to evolve.

The story of Ottawa is one that's defined by myriad things: water travel, explorers, fire, farmers, politicians, working class folk, industry, and much more. Along the way, the city grew slowly from a Victorian lumber town (considered the most dangerous in the British Commonwealth in 1845) into a remarkably clean and green cosmopolitan hub of government, high-tech industry, and the arts. The tech boom in the 1990s (including the launch of both Nortel and Corel) made Ottawa much wealthier and more global in outlook; some feel that its identity as a cutting-edge town is better known internationally than in Canada. Others might say that Ottawa – listed as the seventh coldest world capital – has but two seasons: winter and construction. Okay, some of the stereotypes are true, but there is still plenty of culture, activity, and excitement beyond the snowdrifts, in and around the scaffolding – in places where you might not think to look. And our summers belie the stereotypes of Canadian climate, yielding weeks of blistering muggy days. And regardless of the season, there's always a festival to be found.

Ottawa is a city built on contradictions: green space and concrete; embassies and art galleries; an identity split between that of a national capital and that of a city all its own; a thriving, northern metropolis that includes freaks, weirdoes, and night-owls, alongside the small-"c" conservative types who crawl into bed by 10 p.m. Ottawa can be a city that keeps itself quiet, even to the point of self-deprecation and self-mockery. But there are strange and wonderful things here; you just have to know where to look.

(Note: all phone numbers listed in this book have a 613 area code, unless otherwise noted.)

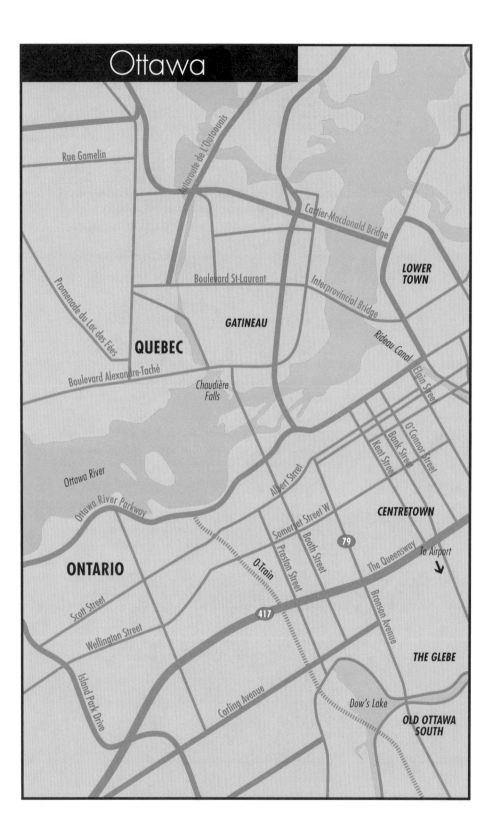

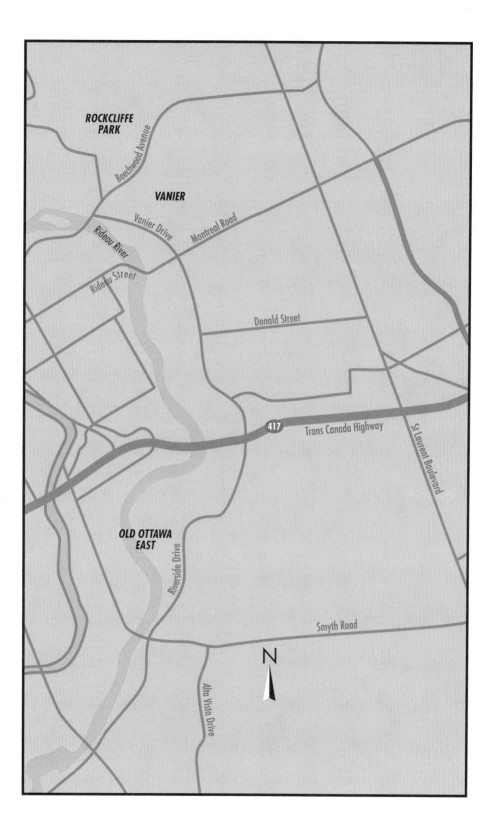

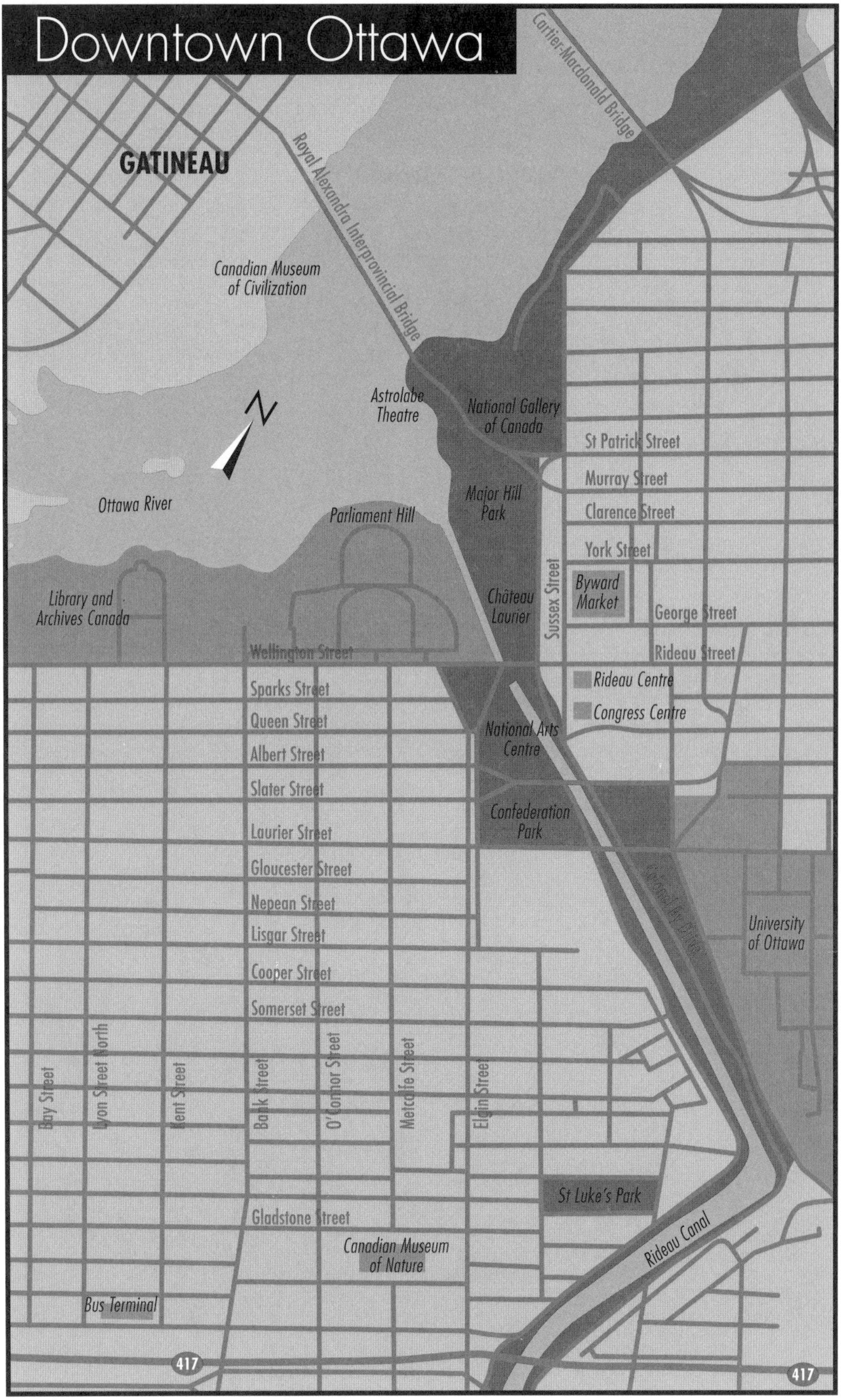

Downtown Ottawa

GATINEAU

Cartier-Macdonald Bridge

Royal Alexandra Interprovincial Bridge

Canadian Museum
of Civilization

Astrolabe
Theatre

National Gallery
of Canada

St Patrick Street

Murray Street

Clarence Street

Major Hill
Park

York Street

Ottawa River

Parliament Hill

Byward
Market

George Street

Library and
Archives Canada

Château
Laurier

Sussex Street

Rideau Street

Wellington Street

Rideau Centre

Sparks Street

Congress Centre

Queen Street

National Arts
Centre

Albert Street

Slater Street

Laurier Street

Confederation
Park

Gloucester Street

Nepean Street

Lisgar Street

University
of Ottawa

Cooper Street

Somerset Street

Bay Street

Lyon Street North

Kent Street

Bank Street

O'Connor Street

Metcalfe Street

Elgin Street

Rideau Canal

St Luke's Park

Gladstone Street

Canadian Museum
of Nature

Bus Terminal

417

417

Landmarks & Destinations

Photo: Tony Tremblay

Ottawa has long been home to a variety of fascinating landmarks and travel destinations. From buildings that are decades old to more recent gems, and from cubbyholes along the Rideau Canal and other secret locations to the treasures offered by the city's numerous neighbourhoods, each with its own character, Ottawa offers a strange and wonderful mixture of big-city trappings and small-town charms.

City on the Ottawa

According to some histories, our city was named to commemorate the bicentenary of an event of historical significance: the opening of the **Ottawa River**, once called Grand River, or the "River of the Algonquins" (as Samuel de Champlain, "the father of New France," called it), or *Kit-chi-sippi* (as the Algonquins themselves named it). In 1654, the French and the Iroquois signed a truce, which accorded the **Peoples of the Big Ears** (the *Outaouais*, an Algonquin tribe) the right to settle along the River of the Algonquins, where they could trade furs to Montreal and live a peaceful existence. The waterway soon became known as *Rivière de l'Outaouais*, the Ottawa River. Two hundred years later – long after the Peoples of the Big Ears (named for the heavy earrings they wore that stretched out their earlobes) had left the area – the citizens of **Bytown**, as the municipality was then called, were seeking selection as the permanent capital of the Province of Canada. They considered the suffix "-*town*" inappropriate for their petition; they wanted a name that carried more significance, something that would reflect the increasing importance of this growing lumber centre. Some of the names considered were **Syndenham** (after Lord Syndenham, Governor of Canada), **Aberdeen** (in honour of George Hamilton-Gordon, Earl of Aberdeen), and **Queensburg** (for Her Majesty Queen Victoria). Others suggested an Aboriginal name would be more appropriate to convey the character of the community. In 1853, Mayor Joseph-Balsora Turgeon obtained the agreement of municipal council to adopt the name of Ottawa to mark the 200th anniversary of the opening of the River of the Algonquins for peaceful navigation by the Outaouais.

Photo: Charles Earl

With the help of local guides, French explorer **Samuel de Champlain** reached the present-day site of Ottawa on June 3, 1613, portaging two days later past Chats Falls on the upper Ottawa (then the Grand River), and paddling along Lac des Chats up to what is now **Arnprior**, **Braeside**, and **Sand Point**. In 1915, a monument to de Champlain – depicting him gazing wisely through an astrolabe – was unveiled at Ottawa's **Nepean Point**, which is behind the **National Gallery of Canada** (just west of Sussex Dr. and St. Patrick St.). Unfortunately, the sculptor Hamilton MacCarthy had de Champlain holding the instrument upside down (it took years for anyone to notice). Nepean Point also boasts a lovely view of the area, including Gatineau, Quebec, and Chaudière Falls. The Astrolabe Theatre (just behind the Gallery; *239-5000*) at the point features a 700-seat amphitheatre and is the scene of concerts and shows throughout the summer.

THE DEPARTMENT OF MISSING MONUMENTS

In 1966, the Department of the Secretary of State proposed four monuments for Parliament Hill. Two of them – tributes to Prime Ministers William Lyon Mackenzie King and Louis St Laurent – were commissioned, and can be easily found on the Hill. But what happened to the other two, built for lesser-known prime ministers of the 20th century, **Arthur Meighen** and **Richard Bedford Bennett**? The first, for Meighen, was completed in 1970 but never received final approval by the government and remained in storage for years before finally being installed in 1987, in Lind Park, in the town of St. Marys, Ontario, the town nearby to his birthplace and where he was eventually buried. The Bennett statue was rejected at the model stage not, as then-Secretary of State Judy LaMarsh explained, for a lack of artistic merit, but because the work wasn't suitable "as representations to future generations of the statesmen of the past." Prime Minister John Diefenbaker's words on the two statues were far more specific, referring to the Meighen statue as "the greatest monstrosity ever produced – a mixture of Ichabod Crane and Daddy Longlegs," and the Bennett model as a "mummy." With these monuments now hidden somewhere in the National Capital Commission storage, it is unclear if replacement statues of the two will ever be commissioned.

CATTLE CASTLE

The **Aberdeen Pavilion** on the Exhibition grounds is named after John Hamilton-Gordon, first Marquess of Aberdeen and Temair, Governor General from 1893 to 1899, and is known informally as the "Cattle Castle." Said to be the last surviving Canadian example of a Victorian exhibition hall (used mostly for agricultural shows), it was used as a military structure during the war, and was the home of Lord Strathcona's Horse (now an armoured regiment of the Canadian Forces) before they left for the Boer War. Designed by Moses Edley and built for the exhibition grounds in 1898, the building survived a fire in 1907 and was scheduled for demolition in 1991, becoming a central issue in the 1991 Ottawa election before it was finally restored in 1992–94. It is now a National Historic Site.

Part of the informal Ottawa-Gatineau region, the **City of Gatineau** (which was, before amalgamation in 2002, called Hull) sits on the Quebec side of the Ottawa River, directly across from Ottawa. Gatineau was founded by American lumber baron **Philemon Wright** in 1800 (making it a few decades older than Ottawa), after he built the first mill at Chaudière Falls. It was originally called Wright's Village, then Wrightsville, then Wrightstown before becoming Hull (named after the original Wright family home town of Kingston-upon-Hull in England). Gatineau is currently home to some 242,000 people (a predominantly francophone population) and boasts a number of notable sites, including the **Museum of Civilization** (see p. 36), **Casino du Lac Leamy** *(1 Boul. du Casino, 819-772-2100, casino-du-lac-leamy. com)*, and the 363 square kilometres of **Gatineau Park** *(canadascapital.gc.ca/gatineau)*, as well as various federal government buildings and a branch of **Library and Archives Canada** *(Preservation Centre, 625 Boul. du Carrefour; see collectionscanada.gc.ca)*.

A Museum Fit for a King

Photo: John W. MacDonald

In addition to part of William Lyon Mackenzie King's legacy as the 10th Prime Minister of Canada are the "fake ruins" he built in the Gatineau Hills of his summer home, which he called "Moorside." Now a museum and historic site, the **Mackenzie King Estate** sits in the midst of Gatineau Park, where he decorated the grounds of his estate with bits from other sites, including the British Bank of North America (demolished in Ottawa in 1936) and the original Parliament Buildings. Future Prime Minister Lester B. Pearson, then a diplomat at Canada House in London, England, was even asked to send him fragments of the bombed Palace of Westminster during World War II. How can you say no to such a request from your wartime PM? Pearson complied, and the pieces were sent back to Canada by submarine. A magnificent sight in the midst of the Gatineau Hills, it's become a haven for wedding parties and photographers. *819-827-2020; follow links for directions and hours at canadascapital.gc.ca*

Small Islands, Big Kettle

Chaudière Falls and **Chaudière Island** sit (along with neighbouring Victoria Island) on the Ottawa River just west of the downtown Ottawa core, where the Booth Street Bridge (also known as the Chandière Bridge) passes from the western end of Centretown into Gatineau. Exploring the area in 1613, Samuel de Champlain originally recorded the Algonquin name for the site of the falls as Asticou, meaning "kettle" or "cauldron," which became translated by the French as La Chaudière (what the English then called "the Big Kettle"). It was considered a sacred place to gather, trade, and celebrate for thousands of years before European arrival.

One of the earliest buildings in the area was built at the foot of the Falls, on the south shore of Nepean Point, where the general store tavern had been constructed by Jehiel Collins in 1809 and soon became known as Collins Landing. The name was later changed to Bellows Landing when Collins sold to Caleb Bellows a few years later, and in 1818, its name was changed again to Richmond Landing (see p. 46).

In the late 1800s, a mill that would produce pulp, paper, and matches was opened at Chaudière Falls and Chaudière Island by Ezra Butler Eddy (yes, the Eddy Matches guy). Over a century later, in 2005, the now Domtar-Eddy site announced mill closings, which meant the city would lose one of the last links to Bytown's beginnings as an important 18th-century lumber town. To this day, rumours persist about transforming the area into a major tourist attraction, opening up the land to the public, and encouraging multiple uses, similar to Vancouver's Granville Island, encompassing historic sites associated with First Nations, early settlers, and industrial pioneers.

Photo: John Woodruff c.1900

Photo: Hanif Bayat

FLAME ON

At one second past midnight on January 1, 1967, Prime Minister Lester B. Pearson launched Canada's centennial by lighting, for the first time, the **Centennial Flame**, informally known as the "eternal flame." The shields surrounding the flame correspond to the years when each province or territory joined Confederation, and the water from the fountain symbolizes Canada's unity from sea to sea. An Act passed by Parliament in 1991 ensures that all the coins thrown into the fountain go to fund research by and about Canadians with disabilities.

WATERY LITERATURE

There was a joke that you weren't a real Ottawa poet around 1900 unless you had written a poem about the Chaudière Falls or Rapids. Who are we to argue with history? In the fall of 2006, one local group (including this author) latched on to the literary significance of the Falls by founding **Chaudiere Books** (chaudierebooks.com).

EMBASSIES OFF
THE BEATEN PATH

Being the nation's capital, Ottawa is home to a variety of international embassies. A good number of them exist in downtown office buildings, but here are a few older embassies that are housed in their own historic sites around the city.

Brunei Darussalam: This large house at 395 Laurier Avenue East was built in 1871 by lumber baron John A. Cameron, who rented it out first to Joseph-Edouard Cauchon, who would become Speaker of the Canadian Senate. His wife named the residence "Stadacona Hall," using the indigenous people's name for Quebec City. Another notable couple who resided here was Sir John A. Macdonald, Canada's first Prime Minister, and his wife. After World War II, the building was purchased by Belgium to house their ambassador, and finally sold in the 1990s for the sake of downsizing to the Government of Brunei, who uses it as its High Commission.

Centretown

Holding a great percentage of what could be called Ottawa's downtown core, Centretown was originally the predominantly Scottish and English Presbyterian ying to Lowertown's French and Irish Catholic yang. Centretown currently contains the **Bank Street Promenade**, **Sparks Street**, the **Golden Triangle** area east of Elgin Street, Ottawa's own **unofficial gay district** (or official, depending on whom you ask), as well as **Little Italy** and **Chinatown** (now called "Somerset Heights"). Some of Centretown's highlights include a spectacular **nightlife** on a number of these main streets, depending on your tastes (see Nightlife chapter). Notable destinations include **Barrymore's Music Hall**, the **Currency Museum**, the **Museum of Nature**, and, of course, the **Parliament Buildings**.

Lowertown

One of the oldest parts of the city, Lowertown (including the **Byward Market**, **Sandy Hill**, and the **University of Ottawa** campus; see photo next page) boasts century-old houses and parks, quiet residential homes, as well as various embassies (France, India, South Africa, Spain), and is the only original part of what is now the City of Ottawa that was originally subdivided for urban development (unlike the Glebe, for example). Lowertown is home to two of the city's founding linguistic communities, French and English, where they have done business side by side for decades. The Lowertown neighbourhood originally constituted the geographic divide between the upper class of New Edinburgh to the immediate east and the residents of the lower income Lowertown, which was predominantly settled by the Irish and French, many of whom arrived to do the grunt work that came with building a city. Lowertown was the flip side of the coin to the predominantly Protestant Uppertown (which explains the three large Catholic churches in close proximity), and became the centre for industrial power in 19th-century Bytown (what Ottawa was called prior to 1855). Many of the French Canadians of Lowertown were lumbermen who had been working for timber magnate Philemon Wright

Photo: Serge Brousseau

across the river in Hull to supply the Rideau Canal with wood and related materials. These workers' homes, unlike the large stone residences that still exist in New Edinburgh and parts of Lowertown, were made of wood and have long since disappeared. Some of the highlights of Lowertown include various outdoor patios, clubs, and restaurants of the Byward Market; used bookstores and shops along **Dalhousie Street**; the **Rideau Centre** (Ottawa's largest downtown shopping centre), the **National Gallery of Canada**, and various commercial art galleries.

The Glebe

Ottawa's oldest neighbourhood, the Glebe was originally surveyed in 1792, but didn't have its first legitimate settler, George Patterson, Chief of the Canal Commissariat, until 1826 (Patterson Creek is named for him, and his house sits at the corner of Canal Street and Patterson Avenue). Predominantly a residential district and bordered by the canal, the Glebe amalgamated into Ottawa against the will of its citizens in the later part of the 19th century, and spent most of the 1980s and 90s becoming extremely gentrified. Home to various eating establishments and outdoor patios, bookstores, and coffeeshops, this area's highlights include the **Glebe Community Centre**, the **Canal Ritz** restaurant, **Carleton University**, **Octopus Books**, and the **SuperEx** fair.

Old Ottawa South

Just below the Glebe (across the bridge over the Rideau, near Lansdowne Park, 1015 Bank Street), Old Ottawa South was, for years, literally the southernmost point in town until the natural growth of the city pushed

France: Acquired in the 1930s, this property at 42 Sussex Drive was once owned by Robert Blackburn, one of New Edinburgh's earliest merchants, a Member of Parliament, a founder of the Ottawa City Passenger Railway Company in 1866, and the man after whom Blackburn Hamlet (a small neighbourhood that currently sits just west of Orléans) was named. Designed by Parisian architect Eugène Beaudouin, the granite structure was built between 1936 and 1939. On the front lawn, in a small artificial pool, sits a miniature of **La Grande Hermione**, explorer Jacques Cartier's ship.

Russia: On New Year's Day, 1956, the building at 285 Charlotte Street caught fire. Despite the fact that the structure was burning brightly, embassy staff refused entry to the fire department, even as officials were desperately removing secret documents from the building. Worried that the fire would spread to adjoining buildings, the fire department persisted. Finally a call was placed to Mayor Charlotte Whitton, who soon arrived at the site. After intense negotiations in the middle of Charlotte Street between the Mayor and the Soviet Ambassador, Dmitri S. Chuvanin, the fire department was finally granted entry, but by then it was far too late.

A few days after the fire, at least half a dozen other ambassadors made a point of telling Whitton that if their embassies caught fire, they would certainly allow entry to the firefighters. Soviet officials moved temporarily to 24 Blackburn Avenue until a new embassy was built on their vacant property, about a year after the fire.

South Africa: In a house built in 1840, this embassy at 15 Sussex Drive sits directly across from the official residence of the Prime Minister. James Stevenson, Bytown's first agent of the Bank of Montreal, lived there for some years, as did industrialist Moss Kent Dickinson, known as "King of the Rideau"; he was also the Mayor of Ottawa from 1864 to 1866.

United States: This monolith at 490 Sussex Drive that blocks the view down Clarence Street toward Parliament Hill was built a few years ago as part of an exchange between the US and Canada. Originally wanting to move the US embassy's new location to somewhere farther outside the downtown area, Canadian officials finally relented and allowed for construction on Sussex Drive after American officials permitted the new Canadian embassy in Washington (which was also outgrowing its previous digs) to take up residence in a particularly attractive historic building they had their eyes on.

what Ottawans consider "south" farther and farther away, now well past where the current O-Train (the city's north-south light rail) stops. Some highlights include the **Ottawa Folklore Centre**, the **Canadian Walk of Fame**, **Patty's Pub**, **Mother Tongue Books**, and a whole slew of antique stores, as well the flea-marketesque **Ottawa Antique Market** (see photo).

Westboro

This neighbourhood has gradually developed into one of the trendiest in the city. Various shops, restaurants, and condos have begun to take over what was previously a lower-income area (including parts of Hintonburg, which was originally developed as a streetcar suburb for downtown civil servants, and Mechanicsville), inching eastward toward the O-Train line and Centretown. Some notable features of the area include **Collected Works Bookstore and Coffeebar**, **Elvis Lives Lane** (behind the infamous Newport Restaurant, see p. 69), and slightly east, into Hintonburg (or "Wellington Village") **The Carleton Tavern**. In 2007, the **Great Canadian Theatre Company** opened their brand new building at the corner of Holland Avenue and Wellington Street.

LeBreton Flats

Captain John LeBreton was a decorated veteran of the War of 1812 who was severely wounded in the Battle of Lundy's Lane (one of the deciding battles in the war). The area now known as LeBreton Flats was named for this war hero, who received a land grant in Bytown on the Ottawa River (where the present-day neighbourhood of Britannia sits, farther west, by Brittania Beach off Carling Avenue). When lands

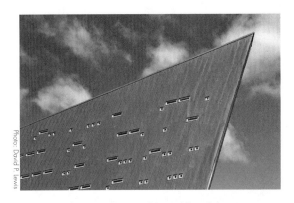
Photo: David P. Lewis

extending from Carling to the middle of the Ottawa and from Bronson Avenue to Booth Street were offered for auction in Brockville, Captain LeBreton bought the whole lot. This angered the Governor General, the Earl of Dalhousie, who refused to buy the land for the Crown at LeBreton's price. Imagine: originally, LeBreton's lands were considered prime for the Rideau Canal project, but LeBreton wanted too much money, moving Dalhousie's plans farther east into Nicholas Sparks' rocky lot (much of what is now home to Centretown from Wellington Street south, including west past current Bronson Avenue and east to the Rideau Canal). This helped Sparks to become the era's only wealthy Irishman in town.

In 1962, the Crown expropriated and bulldozed a portion of LeBreton's land for a vast redevelopment program – that has yet to come to fruition – carving everything away down to Scott and Albert Streets to the south, and cutting Wellington Street off from itself (a sign now hangs in the area for "Old Wellington Street"). Somehow the small residential street known as lower Lorne Avenue, off Albert Street and just below Nanny Goat Hill, survived. In 2006, local residents fought back and won against renewed development, saying that unless the city designated the street a heritage conservation area, the turn-of-the-century homes would give way to suburban-style houses that they insist don't belong there. Thus, the houses on lower Lorne Avenue exist as the only example of what LeBreton Flats used to look like.

In 2004, some development did start to appear, with the newly designed **Canadian War Museum** (see photo above) opening in 2005, and the promise of a series of apartment and government buildings where the Transitway meets Booth Street. But most of what has happened, yet again, is the removal of what was already thriving (a lovely campground, for example).

IT TAKES A VILLAGE

The original village of **Rockcliffe Park**, situated just west of Lowertown and Vanier, belonged to Thomas McKay, the Rideau Canal's contractor; for many years, his widow lived in a stone mansion on the northern boundary of the village. Incorporated as a municipality to preserve its pastoral nature (and to hold back the building boom of the 1920s), it had only a score of permanent homes; otherwise, it was occupied by summer cottages and two private schools, Ashbury College (for boys, established 1910, whose students included actor Matthew Perry, among others), and Elmwood School for girls (established 1915, where author Elizabeth Smart attended). Because of deliberate laws against buildings for any purpose "other than as a single detached family dwelling," there are no apartments or businesses, meaning that there might be a lot of space for kids to play on the streets, but no doctor's offices nor businesses to help pay taxes, which has caused Rockcliffe Park to have some of the highest property tax rates in the city. Despite becoming part of the Regional Municipality of Ottawa-Carleton in 1969, it still retained its status as a village, but was finally amalgamated into the City of Ottawa in 2001.

Sparks Street Mall

The site of the first asphalt laid in the capital in 1895, Sparks Street was named for **Nicholas Sparks** – not the well-known contemporary author who shares the same name, but an illiterate Irish labourer who became Bytown's first tycoon and one of the founding fathers of Ottawa, serving on the first town council in 1847 as well as on the first council of the City of Ottawa. In 1826, he purchased – for £95 – 200 acres of farmland in the heart of the present capital in the area now bounded by Wellington, Rideau, Waller, Laurier, and Bronson streets. He married the widowed daughter of Ottawa lumber baron J. B. Booth and helped raise her nine children, and the land he received as dowry he later sold for the construction of the Rideau Canal (specifically, to then-Governor General, the Earl of Dalhousie).

Sparks Street was opened as a pedestrian mall in 1960, originally on a trial basis. Every few years the city decides to revitalize Sparks Street, without always improving it (in much the way the city tries to do the same with Rideau Street). The city's only pedestrian mall, the city planners spent years changing their minds on whether or not cars should be allowed on the street at all, but they've finally left it alone, and the current mall remains a model for other urban communities in North America (including Washington, DC, and Philadelphia).

Sparks Street Bones

On the morning of March 11, 1977, a Fuller Construction backhoe and crew discovered a damaged skull and the partial remains of two bodies while working an excavation site on Queen Street at Metcalf, right behind the Bank of Commerce building at 62 Sparks Street (now home of Ian Kimmerly Stamps). The police turned the bones over to the coroner, Dr Tom Kendall, who determined that the remains were over a century old, and that the couple in question had died of natural causes. The area had been the site of a graveyard in the 1880s, and officials speculated that the bones had perhaps been disturbed and shifted a number of times during previous excavations. The remains were then collected and reburied.

A STATELY MANOR

One of the earliest and most impressive buildings in Rockcliffe is the **Apostolic Nunciature** (*724 Manor Ave.*), home of the Pope's representative in Canada. The huge structure is reminiscent of an English lord's estate, and comes complete with an arched gate. Assessed at approximately $5.3 million in 2000, the mansion was built in 1838. It was dubbed "Rockcliff" for the limestone cliffs that border the Ottawa River. The village itself was later named in its honour. The mansion, also known as the Rockcliffe Manor House, was purchased by the Holy See in 1962.

Up on the Hill

The Parliament Buildings

Photo: Charles Earl

Thought originally to be an Algonquin camp (given the view of the Ottawa River), the modern site of Parliament Hill would first become a military barrack (Barrack Hill). But when Queen Victoria dubbed Ottawa the Capital of the Province of Canada (a region made up predominantly of Upper Canada and Lower Canada, now Ontario and Quebec) in 1857, construction of the **Parliament Buildings** began. The neo-gothic stone buildings and the spire of the Peace Tower are the heart of political life in Canada, including the **Senate**, the **House of Commons**, and the **Library of Parliament**. The **Peace Tower** houses a 53-bell carillon, a huge clock, and the memorial chamber commemorating Canada's war dead. Through all of this, the seat of Canadian government still sits on disputed Algonquin lands.

In 1916, a huge fire destroyed everything but the library. Construction of the new Parliament Buildings turned out to be plagued by the same problems as the original. Shortages due to World War I, coupled with construction difficulties, delayed the expected completion date by several years

Photo: Charles Earl

BOTTOMS UP!

One of the features of the original Parliament Buildings was a bar directly beneath the House of Commons — with a stairwell leading directly down from the floor of the House — where journalists used to hang out, drinking and keeping tabs on the goings-on of the country.

EXTREME MAKEOVER

When the original Parliament Buildings were constructed, they were well over-budget, and the landscaping was left as a mess of mud for quite some time before the buildings' architect Thomas Fuller was given the go-ahead to start. Inspired by New York's Central Park, the original landscaping included a fountain in front of the tower (that nobody liked). Once Fuller left Ottawa, those in charge of the grounds quickly removed the fountain and replaced it with the eternal flame.

before the government's new digs finally opened in 1920. The new Centre Block was sympathetic in style with the existing buildings on Parliament Hill, but close inspection, especially from the rear where comparisons with the original library are easily made, will reveal the differences. The new building was constructed to be resistant to fire, incorporating intricate stone carvings in place of much of the original wood panelling. As well, since they used soil taken from a landfill across the river, an Aboriginal burial site where the Museum of Civilization currently sits; some say it is entirely possible that the second Parliament Buildings include fragments of Natives' bone in its structure.

Currently housed on Wellington Street, the original Parliament Buildings (both pre- and post-fire versions) were expected to house the entire government of Canada, but with new provinces and new portfolios, the original buildings quickly became too small. The thinking for the subsequent construction was, "the closer the better," with newer foundations broken for the **Confederation Building**, the **Supreme Court**, the **Library and Archives Canada Building**, the **Langevin Block**, the **Bank of Canada**, the **Department of Trade and Commerce**, the **Department of Veterans Affairs**, and the original **United States Embassy**.

There was talk a number of years ago about creating some new buildings on the Hill for the sake of new office space, but the state of disrepair in some of the buildings is so advanced that prominent stonemasons were warning as recently as May 2007 that "without emergency repairs, someone could be killed by falling masonry," and that even a minor earthquake could do permanent damage. They've known about the problem for years (major repairs on the West Block have been going on for some time), but the state of disrepair might simply be overtaking government inaction. Unfortunately, some of the recent government action in the Langevin Block included Prime Minister Stephen Harper lining an entire hallway with portraits of himself, just outside of his office.

For general tourist information, a good place to check while on your way through the Parliament Buildings site, or before you get there, is **Capital Infocentre** at 90 Wellington Street (across from Parliament Hill, 239-5000, canadascapital.gc.ca).

Parliamentary, My Dear Fuller

Born in Bath, England, **Thomas Fuller** was trained in the office of architect James Wilson and was, by his twenties, the designer of the Anglican cathedral in Antigua in the West Indies. By 1855, he had his own firm and designed the town hall at Bradford-on-Avon. Soon after, he won the competition to design the new Parliament Buildings in Ottawa. He later became Chief Architect to the Dominion of Canada, designing hundreds of buildings in Canada and the United States, including the New York State Capitol in Albany, the San Francisco City Hall, and the **All Saints' Anglican Church** at 347 Richmond Road (built in 1865). Fuller died in 1898 and was returned to his family in Ottawa (he was buried in Beechwood Cemetery, see p. 162), where some of his descendants run one of the city's leading construction firms, Thomas Fuller Construction.

Save the Flag

There was a movement in Ottawa to preserve the historic **Peace Tower flag** that managed to survive the 1916 Parliament Hill Fire. Some five years after the fire, it flew temporarily over the new Peace Tower before moving into storage. Needing some $6,000 to restore the withered flag in 2006, the **Bytown Museum** attempted to raise the funds from various levels of government, including directly asking Members of Parliament, but was unsuccessful. Recently, the museum went to the media, saying that even $20 from every Member of Parliament would ensure the flag could be properly conserved and mounted for long-term display. Of course, once the public was made aware of the controversy surrounding the survival of the flag, various

THE LONG JOURNEY OF THE ASTROLABE

It's believed that de Champlain lost his astrolabe, a 17th-century model of the ancient navigational instrument, during a difficult portage through the Cobden area northwest of Ottawa in 1613. The device was lost for centuries until turning up in a farmer's field in the Ottawa Valley, dug up by a plow. Marked "Paris 1603," the instrument was found in 1867 by a young boy who was clearing brush with his father. It was eventually sold to a Toronto businessman, then purchased by an American collector for $500. The new owner willed it to the New York Historical Society upon his death in 1942. Canadian officials worked for years to repatriate the item unsuccessfully until 1989, when the astrolabe finally returned to Ottawa in conjunction with the opening of the **Museum of Civilization** (see p. 36); the Ministry of Communications and Culture paid the American Museum a "token" fee of $250,000. It now holds pride of place at the Museum of Civilization in Gatineau, just across the Ottawa River from the statue on Nepean Point. Some question the authenticity of the object, but apparently there are only 35 such surviving astrolabes from the 17th century like the one de Champlain used.

MPs and senators, as well as members of the public, donated roughly $5,000 to help. The flag has since been restored and is currently on display in the Bytown Museum.

Photo: John W. MacDonald

THE MILL BENEATH THE HILL

It may seem odd now, but at one point there was a steam-powered lumber mill just at the shore of the Ottawa River below Parliament Hill. Built sometime in the early 1870s (perhaps even as early as the 1850s), it seems to have quietly vanished by the early 1900s, but has certainly left its traces at water level. Roughly 40 feet wide and 60 feet deep with a smoke-stack that towered about 60 feet high, you can still find traces of the original building, including a subsurface passageway with arches that might have been part of the steam boiler system, and the stone base of the smoke-stack. The site is now used as an ad-hoc camping area complete with broken bottles, a firepit, and the occasional abandoned sleeping bag.

Boom!

Manufactured in England in 1807 and purchased by the Postmaster General for $250.45, the nine-pound muzzle loader **Noon Gun** was originally authorized to fire a daily single round to mark the stroke of noon, enabling post office clerks to maintain mail service on a correct schedule. First used as a ship's cannon, it was donated by the British Army to the British Garrison in Canada as a souvenir of the Crimean War, and was placed on Parliament Hill between the East Block and the Parliamentary Library. Its first signal was fired at noon on April 26, 1869. Following the fire of 1916, the gun was removed to Major's Hill Park, and is now fired daily off Nepean Point at noon, Monday through Saturday, and at 10 a.m. on Sundays, Christmas Day, New Year's Day, Good Friday, and Thanksgiving Day, so as not to disturb nearby congregations. One notable misfire occurred in 1966, when the appointed gunner arrived to find the gun missing. It was soon retrieved by the RCMP, who discovered that boisterous students had made off with it as a prank, intending to wheel it out as the star attraction in a winter carnival parade.

Sir Galahad of Wellington Street

Are you wondering why there is a statue of Sir Galahad directly in front of the grounds of Parliament Hill? Well, here's the story: Lady Minto, wife of Canada's Governor General at the turn of the 20th century (who later founded the **Minto Skating Club** in 1903), hosted a series of weekly skating parties at Rideau Hall, giving the sport a tremendous boost. At one of these outings, in 1901, Miss Bessie Blair, daughter of the Minister of Railways and Canals, and her skating partner fell through the ice on the Ottawa River near the mouth of the Gatineau River. Fortunately, Blair's companion escaped, but the attempt by government employee Henry Albert Harper to rescue Miss Blair failed, and both were lost. To acknowledge both Harper's bravery and the loss of such a close friend, William Lyon Mackenzie King, in the days before he became prime minister, commissioned a statue of Sir Galahad, known as "the pure." A confirmed bachelor his whole life (if you don't count his spiritual advisors or his faithful dog, who he thought was a reincarnation of his departed mother), Mackenzie King had many close friends, both male and female, but apparently Harper was especially close, leading to a particular kind of rumour around town. Perhaps this statue can be considered a tribute to Mackenzie King's knight in shining armour.

TWENTY-STOREY TIMEPIECE

Finally completed in 2005 after more than a decade of construction, the 20-storey **World Exchange Plaza** takes up the entire block between Metcalf and O'Connor Streets south of Queen Street, housing a variety of companies including CTV, Microscoft, and TD Canada Trust, and is home to a shopping mall and a movie theatre, as well as life-size models of narwhales and belugas hanging from the ceiling. If you don't have a watch and can't tell the time by looking at the sun, you can always watch the ball on top of the World Exchange.

EXPENSIVE ART

It might be illegal to tear up American currency, but not Canadian cash. For years Ottawa artist Marc Adornato has been making artwork out of torn Canadian currency, including an image of a Canadian flag made up of $2,000 worth of $50 and $100 bills, and regularly tears up money at parties. Some of his work has been shown at the **Currency Museum** where, according to urban legend, the largest gold deposit in the world is located in the Bank of Canada vaults under Wellington Street.
245 Sparks St., 782-8914, bank-banque-canada.ca; free admission — yes, free!

Rideau Canal

Photo: Charles Earl

AN EMPTY REGISTRY

Known as the **Old Registry Office**, that little building on the west side of the Rideau Centre at 70 Nicholas Street was erected in 1873 and used as the city registry until 1909. Eventually, it was sold to the federal government in 1935 and has remained empty and unused now for years. One of only four of its kind left in Ontario, it remains an understated but impressive example of Victorian architecture, with barrel-vaulted ceiling and outside adornments. The Registry was later sold to the Viking-Rideau Corporation in the 1990s without any stipulation that the building had to be preserved, and there has been talk of moving or even destroying it so the Rideau Centre and the Ottawa Congress Centre can be expanded. For a while, literary historian Steve Artelle was in talks with the city to let the Ottawa Literary Heritage Society use the space as a museum, but so far, nothing has come of it.

Perhaps the most famous site in the City of Ottawa, the **Rideau Canal** is considered one of the greatest engineering feats of the 19th century. It was originally commissioned for the War of 1812 (Canada is the only country to have successfully held back an American invasion) so ship traffic (predominantly British troops) could travel from Montreal to Kingston, Ontario, thus bypassing the American border on the south shore of the St Lawrence River. The construction of the Canal was overseen by **Lieutenant-Colonel John By**, of the British Royal Engineers, who gave his name to the original town of Bytown, but later died in England in shame due to the accusation (unfounded) that he had "carelessly overspent" to build the Canal. (The man who replaced him, Major Daniel Bolton, took up residence in By's house on Barrack's Hill, which was later renamed **Major's Hill Park** in his honour.) Part of the problem was the colossal amount of bedrock that the builders had to blast their way through, from the canal mouth to Dow's Swamp (what became Dow's Lake). The Rideau Canal and Rideau Waterway is 202 kilometres (125 mi) long with 47 masonry locks and 52 dams that connect the Ottawa River with lower parts of the St Lawrence Seaway to provide safe passage between what was then Upper and Lower Canada.

For strategic reasons, Sleigh Bay, renamed Entrance Bay, was chosen as the starting point of the canal on the Ottawa River, helping make landowner Nicholas Sparks a wealthy man (location, location, location, they always say), and the site became the hub around which Bytown was built. Construction occurred between 1826 and 1832 with a work force of French-Canadian and British stonemasons and Irish labourers (many of whom lived in mud huts in Cork Town, along the river just west of the downtown core) who built this wonder of engineering to Kingston, Ontario.

On May 29, 1832, the Rideau Canal was opened to traffic, at a cost of £800,000. The Rideau Canal was officially designated a UNESCO World Heritage Site in 2007.

Remains of the Day

In 2006, workers who were draining the Rideau Canal in preparation for the winter skating season discovered a bag of human bones. Identified as belonging to a woman between 35 and 45 years old who was killed one year before, the remains were found in a mesh sack in the canal near Bronson Avenue. Police suspected foul play, speculating that the teeth and jawbone that were missing were deliberately removed in order to mask identification. Police had hoped that DNA evidence would provide some sort of lead; there are several unsolved cases of women gone missing in Ottawa. This particular case, however, remains unsolved as well.

Keep Your Eyes Peeled

Along the Rideau Canal, on a building at the University of Ottawa, there's a very large and intriguing mural, black on white, depicting a single pair of eyes. The late **James Boyd**, a self-taught artist from Scotland who came to Canada as a young lad, painted the massive mural that is situated on the west wall of **Macdonald Hall** (150 Louis Pasteur St.), in the 1970s. An active artist and professor in the fine arts department of the University of Ottawa, Boyd was for years one of Ottawa's most important visual artists, showing work nationally and internationally. Various rumours abound that the mural's eyes are those of Prime Minister Pierre Trudeau, or Trudeau's rival René Lévesque, or even the artist's own girlfriend.

This is not the only piece of public art Boyd created during his long career: you can also find, as part of the City of Ottawa's fine art collection, *The Worthy Thane of Ross*, a mixed media embossed work on display at the **Canterbury Community Centre** (2185 Arch St., 738-8998), and a three-part series of coloured etchings,

A FEW CANAL FACTS:

• In 1827, the infamous Captain **John Franklin**, who would later perish on an unsuccessful expedition to find the Northwest Passage, laid a 1.25-tonne cornerstone at the third lock in the entrance to the Canal.

• The village of **Newboro** (since renamed Newborough) in Ontario's Leeds County was founded by Rideau Canal workers in 1830.

• The previous incarnation of the **Chaudière Bridge** (which now connects Booth Street to Gatineau) was the Union Bridge which connected Bytown to the small community of Hull to help bring supplies from Montreal for the building of the Canal. The ceremonial first stone was laid by Lord Dalhousie, who had authorized the construction of the bridge at the foot of Chaudière Falls. And in 1828, floodwaters severely damaged the bridge, enough that the entire bridge was swept away, killing one person in the process.

• **Dow's Lake**, a man-made lake along the Canal that serves as the southern-most end of the Canal's enormous outdoor ice-skating rink and focal point of February's **Winterlude** (see p. 157) activities that happen around the city, was originally an area known as Dow's Great Swamp.

Photo: John W. MacDonald

called *Eumenides, Sunrise and Yellow Attack* at the **Overbrook-Forbes Community Resource Centre** *(225 Donald St., 745-0073)*.

The Fairmont Château Laurier

One of the original Canadian Pacific hotels built at the advent of the national rail line, The Fairmont Château Laurier *(1 Rideau St., 241-1414, Fairmont.com/laurier)*, like many other such hotels in the country, was built in close proximity to the original Ottawa train station (now the Conference Centre). Commissioned in 1907 by American-born railwayman Charles Melville Hays, the hotel emulated the French Renaissance style, using granite blocks for the base, buff Indiana limestone for the walls, and copper for the roof (a few years ago, the

copper was replaced, giving the heart of downtown a temporary reflective glow, before oxidizing darker brown to what will become, again, green). Unfortunately, days before the scheduled opening of the hotel in 1912, Hays was returning from England – with new dining room furniture in tow – aboard the RMS *Titanic*; yes, *that Titanic*. Hays perished, and rumours abound of his ghost still wandering the halls of the hotel.

Walk through the basement and you can see a display of captioned photos telling the story of some of the hotel's (and Ottawa's) early history, including Hays' *Titanic* crossing. This is where U2 might stay when they come

IN MEMORY OF ...

In 2004, a **Celtic cross memorial** was unveiled on the east side of the lower locks to honour the near-thousand labourers – most of Irish descent – who died during the construction of the Rideau Canal. (A similar cross stands near Kingston, at the other end of the canal.) The five symbols on the cross represent the explosion, the mosquito, the wheelbarrow, the shovel and pick, and the harp.

A NEARBY RETREAT

It was once said that there were tunnels going from the Château Laurier to Parliament Hill. Canada's first prime minister, John A. MacDonald, a notorious booze hound, was said to have had a permanent room at the hotel in case he was too drunk to make it home (it was once dubbed "the third chamber of Parliament" for the number of politicians roaming its corridors, and even became Prime Minister R. B. Bennett's official residence for five years).

to town, or various visiting diplomats; hang around the lobby and see who walks by. Some of the guests over the years have included Shirley Temple, Nelson Eddy, Billy Bishop, Roger Moore, Bryan Adams, Karen Kain, Harry Belafonte, Nelson Mandela, and Marlene Dietrich.

Come Back, Shane!

American actor Alan Ladd – famous for his starring role in the 1953 western *Shane*, and for being father-in-law to Cheryl (from the original *Charlie's Angels* TV show) – stayed at the Château Laurier in the early 1950s while re-doing dialogue for the film *Saskatchewan* (1954). While he was here, he broke his ankle capering in the pool – the apparent result of an attempt to entertain his daughter. If you want, you can swim in their art deco pool yourself and see where Ladd did it, for only 20 dollars.

The People's University

Looking at the unassuming apartment complex now, who would've known that a college once existed here at 160 Chapel Street? Known as the "People's University," **Pestalozzi College** was a student-run cooperative residence that existed in the late 1960s and into the 70s as a free-thinking, open-concept school, based on the model of Toronto's infamous student-run Rochdale College. Some of the extracurricular activities that occurred in the building included literary readings and the Ontario Provincial Gay Liberation Conference in 1973 as well as Ottawa's first public gay dance, hosted by GO (Gays of Ottawa, who also had their headquarters there). Existing as an alternative school, the entire building was a strange mix of open education, residence, and "free love and good drugs" that eventually fell apart in much the same way that Rochdale did. By the late 1970s, both school and building existed as a community centre of sorts, offering facilities for artists' studios and yoga classes before the entire building (with very little notice) was converted by its owners into an apartment complex, Horizon Towers. A holdover from the Pestalozzi days, the **Sitar Indian Restaurant** on the ground floor still exists (*417 Rideau St., 789-7979*).

PM'S PAD

Laurier House *(335 Laurier Ave. E., 992-8142)* is the former residence of not one but two of Canada's prime ministers (**Sir Wilfred Laurier** and **Mackenzie King**). Now a museum, the house also recreates the study of another PM, **Lester B. Pearson**, winner of the Nobel Peace Prize. Full of authentic books, furnishings, and memorabilia, the room displays the crystal ball Pearson once received as a gift. Open Tuesday to Sunday, closed January 1, Good Friday, and December 25, operated by Parks Canada.

OPEN HOUSES

Since 2002, one of the highlights of spring has been **Doors Open** Ottawa, when dozens of embassies, places of worship, apartment buildings, museums, and other historic and heritage buildings participate in the largest architectural and heritage event in the city. Get access to some spaces you probably wouldn't have been able to otherwise. Follow the links to Doors Open at *ottawa.ca.*

The majestic **Rideau Hall** (perched on a site that overlooks the Ottawa and Rideau Rivers) was originally an 11-room house that Scottish stonemason Thomas McKay built for himself and his family in the 1830s. Thirty years later, the federal government leased the house, along with 80 acres of adjacent "McKay's bush," for Governor General Viscount Monck and his household prior to their arrival in Ottawa. Upon Confederation, the house was purchased as the official residence of the Governor General, and underwent extensive renovations, including a new wing, conservatory, and, later on, an entrance lodge in 1868, a new ballroom in the early 1870s, and the rebuilding of the entire façade in 1910. Originally known only informally as "Rideau Hall" (Lady Stanley, wife of Governor General Lord Stanley, was chastised by Queen Victoria in 1889 for using the informal name instead of the official "Government House"), the name has stuck, and the building is commonly known by both titles. The present building boasts 60 rooms, some on display during summer tourist season. Unfortunately, since the capital was seen as a desolate and cultural backwater for many years, it was also where several early Governor General residents were heard complaining about their stay; fortunately for the mood of the surrounding city, there hasn't been any equivalent complaining for decades.

The Family Business

Said to be originally a hardware store by some and a grocery store by others, the building at the corner of Bank and Lisgar Streets has had an uncertain history. Built in the early 1900s, it's currently the main location for **Wallack's Art Supplies** (*231 Bank St., 234-1800, wallacks.com*). This family enterprise was originally opened in 1939 in another location by Samuel Wallack. His son John moved the business into its current address in 1977, and it now boasts eight stores around Ottawa, Gatineau, and Kingston, as well as **Wallack's Gallery** (*203 Bank St., 235-4339, wallackgalleries.com*) just down the street. Upstairs from Wallack's main location is **Invisible Cinema** (*391 Lisgar St., 237-0769*), a gallery space that doubles as a video and DVD rental outlet, where you'll find some of the best offbeat titles you can't usually find at the big chain stores. Their current space previously housed the artist-run centre **Gallery 101**, and before that a bookstore space owned and operated by the late Ottawa writer and photographer **Richard Simmons** (no, not *that* Richard Simmons), who was also a curator at the Vancouver Art Gallery in the 1960s. Simmons was not only known as the first curator of a public space to purchase work by Greg Curnoe, but he was also around for the beginnings of *3-Cent Pulp* (the pamphlet published by Pulp Press in the 1970s), and he even published a novel, *Sweet Marie*.

The Museum Crawl

Canadian Museum of Nature

Housed in the **Victoria Memorial Museum Building** (VMMB) on the corner of Metcalf and McLeod Streets, the Canadian Museum of Nature (*240 McLeod St., 566-4700 or 1-800-263-4433, nature.ca*) was built on top of a 140-foot-thick layer of clay. It has been plagued with problems since its inception – most notably, the lack of a firm foundation caused the building to settle almost immediately after construction began (causing many of the labourers to refuse to work in the basement). The building contractors knew of the unsuitability of the location, but the government insisted they continue. Painstakingly built over the course of seven years, the

AN APOTHECARY BURIAL SITE?

Due to all the **Aboriginal burial sites** said to be in the area by the Ottawa River (the Museum of Civilization is said to be built on one), pre-construction of the new Canadian War Museum included a geological survey of the ground before anything could be built. Instead of finding any Aboriginal remains or artifacts, however, a number of beer bottles were discovered (there was once a brewery at nearby Preston and Scott Streets), and even some turn-of-the-century drug paraphernalia, including morphine.

SCOUTS CANADA

ARE YOU PREPARED?

Ottawa is home to the **Museum of Canadian Scouting**, located at the Scouts Canada headquarters, featuring displays that depict the history of Canadian scouting and exhibits on the life of Lord R.S.S. Baden-Powell, founder of the Boy Scouts, including pertinent documents, photographs and artifacts.
1345 Baseline Rd., 224-5131, scouts.ca

LA GROTTE NOTRE-DAME DE LOURDES

Now surrounded by apartment buildings and townhouse complexes, the Notre-Dame de Lourdes church on Montreal Road was founded in 1887 by the residents of the former community of Janeville as a pilgrimage destination before moving to its current location (*435 Montreal Rd., 741-4175*) in 1910. Its current location exists as a sanctuary in the midst of urban sprawl, in the francophone district of Vanier.

Photo: John W. MacDonald

Designed as a Canadian counterpart to the major Christian pilgrimage site Our Lady of Lourdes Basilica in the French Pyrenees, the landscape includes an artificial grotto of rocks and cement shelters, statues of the Virgin Mary and St Bernadette (think of Leonard Cohen), and a small altar. Unfortunately, a fire destroyed the original building on this site in 1973 (luckily no one was injured), but it was quickly rebuilt; you can currently see a large altar hold pride of place in the front – a statue of Calvary, and various plaques dating back to 1927.

museum was officially opened in 1912. When fire destroyed the original Parliament buildings in 1916, the VMMB was used to convene the House of Commons and Parliament for the five years before the opening of the rebuilt Parliament Buildings. The VMMB was also the only building to suffer any significant damage during the Ottawa earthquake of 1925, when the arches on all four floors cracked at their apexes, and plaster fell from the ceilings. Considering the years the museum has spent constructing interior structural barriers to keep such an event from shaking the old building apart, staff and visitors should consider themselves lucky the whole structure didn't fall in on them at the time. Director of Exhibition Services Monty Reid has suggested, with more recent excavation uncovering some bricked-in doorways, that the rumours of tunnels running from the museum's sub-basements heading north (connecting to an unknown and long-forgotten end) might have some basis in fact.

Over the past few years, the museum – with many life-size displays of wild mammals, birds, and dinosaurs (both full-sized skeletons and "fleshed-out" versions) – has embarked on an extensive renewal project that will continue until 2010, with a completely renovated building and new galleries. The best time to visit is on a Tuesday afternoon, when the space is relatively empty of visitors, and you can let smaller children run around.

The woolly mammoth outside is always a favourite, or you can check out the upper floors, and see if you can catch a sighting of the ghosts that reputedly haunt the space. Free admission on special days; tour rates are also available, including guided and unguided, with reservations. Winter hours (September 4–April 30) Tuesday to Sunday, 9 a.m.–5 p.m., Thursdays until 8 p.m. and Mondays closed (with holiday exceptions); summer hours (May 1–September 3) open daily 9 a.m.–6 p.m., Wednesdays and Thursdays until 8 p.m.

Another part of the Canadian Museum of Nature is the **Natural Heritage Building**, which houses the museum's collection, library, and most of its administrative offices *(1740 Pink Rd., Gatineau)*. Although only the library is open to the public, the website includes an online catalogue *(geoweb.nature.ca:8003)*. It rightly boasts one of the oldest natural history collections in Canada, tracing its beginnings to 1842 with the formation of the **Geological Survey of Canada**. With more than 35,000 titles, 2,000 periodical titles, and a rare book collection, the library also includes museum publications, cartographic materials, manuscripts, and much, much more. Open Monday to Friday, 8:30 a.m.–4:30 p.m. (closed Saturdays, Sundays, and holidays).

Canadian War Museum

In its new building just off LeBreton Flats that opened in 2005, the Canadian War Museum features an

array of items, including one of Hitler's cars, 19th-century artillery pieces, tanks, and a variety of other artifacts. The museum showcases not only Canada's military history during times of war, but also how the military helped shape the country itself. One of the highlights of the new building

CANADIAN MUSEUM OF CIVILIZATION

Across the river in Gatineau (just across from **Nepean Point** and the **National Gallery of Canada**) is the Canadian Museum of Civilization *(100 Laurier St., 819-776-7000 or 800-555-5621, civilization.ca)*, established to illustrate Canada's history and heritage over 1,000 years of settlement. Some of the permanent attractions include the **Children's Museum**; the world's first convertible **IMAX/Omnimax** theatre; the **Canada Hall**, a setting for many life-size reconstructions from Canada's past; and the **Grand Hall**, an expansive space housing six Pacific Coast indigenous houses and hosting a variety of demonstrations, First Nations ceremonies, and participatory activities.

OTHER MUSEUMS & HISTORIC SITES

The Billings Estate Museum & Billings Bridge

See Ottawa history depicted through the lives of two of the original (and two of the most important and successful) founding settlers of the city, Braddish and Lamira Billings, who established a community circa 1813 near what is now Billings Bridge. *2100 Cabot St., 247-4830, friendsofbillingsestatemuseum.org*

Canada Aviation Museum

Holds the most extensive aviation collection in Canada and one of the best aviation museums in the world. Plans are currently underway to celebrate 100 years of Canadian flight in 2009. *11 Aviation Pkwy, 993-2010, avaiation.technomuses.ca*

Canada Science & Technology Museum

Includes rockets, trains, and everything that sparks, shines, or lights up. *1867 St Laurent Blvd., 991-3044 or 866-442-4416, sciencetech.technomuses.ca*

Canadian Museum of Contemporary Photography

Part of the National Gallery of Canada, the CMCP (*1 Rideau Canal, 990-8257, cmcp.gallery.ca*) sits in part of the original Ottawa train station between the Rideau Canal and the Fairmont Château Laurier. The attractive gallery – with a few too many stairs! – houses a collection of over 160,000 photographic works from the past 40 years. Open Wednesday to Sunday, 10 a.m.–5 p.m., Thursday to 8 p.m. (Note: at the time of publication, the CMCP was closed for major renovations, so it is best to call or check the website prior to your visit.)

is **Memorial Hall**, designed to directly illuminate the headstone of the **Unknown Soldier** with sunlight each Remembrance Day at 11 a.m. A few weeks before the new building opened, one of its War of 1812-era guns – a Henry model 1808 Contract pistol – went missing from an open display case. After some media attention suggested an inside job, and the director of the museum encouraged the thief to return the item, "no questions asked," the gun mysteriously reappeared a week later, hidden in a crate of other materials. As the police fingerprinted all the staff, working through more than 150 suspects who had access to the area, a couple of out-of-town workers simply never showed up again, not even to collect their last paycheques (who can say if any of this is related). Not that it would have been an easy item to get rid of. Worth up to $5,000, a flintlock pistol isn't something you can drop off at the pawnshop. *1 Vimy Pl., 819-776-8600 or 800-555-5621, warmuseum.ca*

Bytown Museum

Toward the locks, just down from the Fairmont Château Laurier and the Canadian Museum of Contemporary Photography is the Bytown Museum *(234-4570, bytownmuseum.com)*, run by the **Historical Society of Ottawa**. Built during the winter of 1826–27 as the treasury and storehouse during the construction of the Rideau Canal, the museum is located in what is considered the oldest existing building in Ottawa, formally presented by the city to the Women's Canadian Historical Society (precursor to the Historical Society) by Mayor Charlotte Whitton in 1951. The Historical Society, which currently meets monthly at the Routhier Community Centre in Lowertown, maintains over 1,500 volumes on early Bytown and Ottawa history in the museum. The reference library is available to the public, and open every Wednesday and Thursday between 10 a.m. and 2 p.m.– it is advised that you call ahead to confirm the librarian is available. The museum itself hosts regular programming throughout the year, including Winterlude events, Haunted March Break, and Canada Day tours; the website grants users a virtual tour if you can't make it there in person.

Lest We Forget

In 1925, a worldwide competition was held to solicit designs for the **National War Memorial** to commemorate those who had served in the armed forces during World War I. With the majority of entries from Canada, there were also applicants from around the world. The winner, a piece by Vernon March of England, was chosen from among 127 entries. March began work on the memorial in England, but he died in 1930 before completing it. The work passed to his sister and six brothers, who completed the bronze figures (including a group of soldiers pulling guns, and figure of an angel) in 1932; they were then displayed in Hyde Park in London for six months in 1933, as the Ottawa site was being prepared. In 1937, the figures were moved overseas; assembly of the entire structure was completed in 1938. About 100,000 people attended the address by King George VI at the official opening on in 1939. The memorial was expanded in 1982 in honour of Canadians who had served in all wars. *Confederation Square, Parliament Buildings*

The Diefenbunker

In 1959, when the Canadian government began digging a massive hole in a farmer's field near Carp just west of Ottawa, it claimed that it was for an army signals installation (no one believed them); in actual fact, it was a four-level, underground emergency government headquarters. Opened in 1961 as an emergency shelter in the event of a nuclear war, it was designed to resist an indirect five-megaton blast (probably why it is out of town), and was built on a five-foot-deep gravel

THE UNKNOWN SOLDIER

In 2000, a Canadian Forces aircraft flew to France to bring the Unknown Soldier (an unidentified soldier from a cemetery in the vicinity of Vimy Ridge, the site of the famous World War I battle in which Canadian soldiers played a large role) back to Canada. Created by British Columbian artist Mary-Ann Liu, the current **Tomb of the Unknown Soldier** sits at the National War Memorial on Elgin and Sparks Streets; it is patterned after the stone altar of the Vimy Memorial but, due to Canada's harsher climate, is made of bronze.

UP THE RIVER

In the mood for a historical daytrip? Drive 90 minutes south along Bank Street to the St Lawrence River and the village of Morrisburg to see **Upper Canada Village**. Recreated from buildings forced to move due to the Long Sault hydroelectric project that flooded a good part of the area in the 1950s, the village depicts life as it would have been in this part of the world in the 1850s. Some highlights include the Union Cheese Factory,

Willard's Hotel, the School House, Physician's House, Blacksmith Shop, Flour Mill, Bakery, and the Gazette Printing Office. On May 2, 1660, in an area that later became Long Sault, **Adam Dollard des Ormeaux** brutally halted the Iroquois advance on Montreal.

13740 County Rd. 2, Morrisburg, 1-800-437-2233, uppercanadavillage.com

CATTLE CASTLE

The **Aberdeen Pavilion** on the Exhibition grounds is named after John Hamilton-Gordon, first Marquess of Aberdeen and Temair, Governor General from 1893 to 1899, and is known informally as the "Cattle Castle." Said to be the last surviving Canadian example of a Victorian exhibition hall (used mostly for agricultural shows), it was used as a military structure during the war, and was even the home of Lord Strathcona's Horse (now an armoured regiment of the Canadian Forces) before they left for the Boer War. Designed by Moses Edley, and built for the exhibition grounds in 1898, the building survived a fire in 1907 and was even scheduled for demolition in 1991, becoming a central issue in the 1991 Ottawa election before it was finally restored in 1992–94. It is now a National Historic Site.

pad that would allow the whole building to shift during the explosion (even the boiler and the air conditioner were mounted on top of giant shock absorbers). Once it became public, it was informally dubbed the "Diefenbunker" by the media in honour of the presiding Prime Minister John Diefenbaker. It stood at the ready for more than 30 years, a 100,000-square-foot outpost complete with hospital, morgue, Bank of Canada vault, and CBC studio. In its 30 years of operation, the only PM who ever visited it was Pierre Trudeau. The shelter was decommissioned in 1994 and became the **Cold War Museum** in 1998; museum guides, many of them former bunker workers, take visitors on a 90-minute tour of the site. Other events have included exhibitions of Cold War-themed art (including work by Ottawa artist Adrian Göllner), a film club, and a lecture series. No cameras. Visits by reserved, guided tours only. Check website for hours and tour start times.
2911 Carp Rd., 839-0007 or 1-800-409-1965, diefenbunker.ca

Ex-cellent

Originally launched at the Central Canada Exhibition in 1888 as an agricultural fair, the **SuperEx** (*ottawasuperex.com*) is Ottawa's 11-day summer exhibition held in August, featuring concerts, midway attractions, animal exhibits (including dog and cat shows), and a variety of free entertainment. While you're there, check out the Aberdeen Pavilion, as old as the Ex itself. When the Rolling Stones visited Ottawa for the first time in 40 years, the 2005 SuperEx boasted an attendance record of 43,000 people at the concert, with a total attendance of almost 600,000. Lansdowne Park also hosts various events throughout the year, including

large concerts (notables in recent years: R. E. M. and Depeche Mode), conventions of all sorts, and a number of doomed football franchises, including the late Ottawa Rough Riders and Ottawa Renegades. Every couple of years, the city threatens to expel the Ex from its current location to outside the city core, but so far it hasn't happened.

Photo: Chris Topp

Transportation

Photo: Charles Earl

Being on the Ottawa River, it seems pretty obvious that water transport was part of how the city was first established, even as it was later developed as a rail town. Since then, Ottawans have figured out a whole bunch of ways to get around, from airplane to car to bicycle, and perhaps a few that you wouldn't expect.

Planes, Trains, and Funeral Processions

Charles Lindbergh – famous for making the first solo, nonstop trans-Atlantic flight – piloted his intrepid *Spirit of St. Louis* to Ottawa in 1927 to join the celebration of Canada's Diamond Jubilee. Escorted to Ottawa by members of the 27th Squadron of the First Pursuit Group of the US Army Air Corps, Lindbergh and his aerial entourage were greeted over Ottawa by three RCAF planes. Unfortunately, after Lindbergh landed on a field near the Ottawa Hunt Club, one escort plane collided with another, forcing the pilot to eject and parachute too close to the ground, killing him. Prime Minister Mackenzie King personally arranged for a funeral, and the body lay in state in the East Block of the Parliament Buildings before being taken to Union Station to be carried aboard a special train to the US for burial. Lindbergh flew over the train as it left the station, scattering peonies from his plane above the coach.

Take the O-Train

Using on preexisting tracks that once went from Hull to what is now Ottawa South, the O-Train runs from downtown at the Bayview station, located under the Wellington and Transitway overpasses (some of it formerly the J. B. Booth rail line, the Transitway is a predominantly east-west, bus-only route that works its way through the city), south down to the Greenboro station located near the South Keys Shopping Centre at Bank Street and Johnston Road. When the light-rail transit system was launched, Ottawa artist Tom Fowler joked that the city should have promoted the train by having the early 2000s boy-band O-Town perform at every stop. (Besides, what else have they got going on

Photo: Charles Earl

these days?) There has been talk about constructing an east-west light-rail line, but there are few places where it could be built without disrupting core traffic for months during construction.

Almost every proposal for extending the O-Train has been considered, promoted, and planned, but to date little action has taken place. In 2006, one report claimed that the new commuter light-rail lines would tear east-west through the Experimental Farm (see p. 25), moving or cutting down trees and other memorials that were planted as dedications to deceased family members. Other reports proposed having the bus-only Transitway replaced with train lines, since most of the downtown routes were originally put in place for the sake of the rail, but by January of 2007, the idea, caught in the wheels of bureaucracy, was as dead as the dodo.

O-Train tickets can be purchased at the stations. They cost $2.25, children under 11 can ride free; you can use the O-Train ticket to transfer to a bus.

Bus Bargains

Regular trips on the OC Transpo buses are $3 cash, or if you use the OC Transpo tickets, which are 95¢ each, you only need two tickets for one adult fare (saving you $1.10!), and only one ticket per ride for children, with five and under free; your proof of payment can also be used for the O-Train. A day pass costs $6.50 prepaid from an official vendor, or $7.25 on the bus, and it even doubles as a family pass if you use it on a Sunday or statutory holiday. Monthly and annual passes are also available.

For complete transit information: *741-4390, octranspo .com.*

Early Train Stations

Ottawa's **first train station** was built in the New Edinburgh neighbourhood by the Bytown & Prescott Railway Company in the mid-1800s, followed by a second at Broad Street. By the early 1880s, more stations opened on Elgin Street, and in 1898, another terminal was created at the corner of Nicholas Street and Mann Avenue. For a number of years, Ottawa appeared to be a nexus of rail traffic, with lines run by many local and national rail corporations snaking through town. In 1910, the government donated a parcel of the Rideau Canal Reserve to the Grand Trunk Railway to build a new, more central, Union Station and a hotel (the Château Laurier).

ART IN TRANSIT

Be on the lookout for commissioned artwork by the late visual artist **Mark Marsters** on the rock face along the number **95, 97, and 86 bus routes**. In one of their few inspired moments, the City of Ottawa commissioned a series of artists for works in public places. Check out the maps by **Adrian Göllner**, for example, just south of Billings Bridge.

RAIL REMOVALS

Ottawa was once a city with a flourishing rail system. It was rail that essentially killed the Rideau Canal water traffic (the whole purpose of the Canal being built). In the grand transportation food chain, it was then the automobile that killed off rail. By the end of World War II, there were 150 railway crossings in the City of Ottawa, and an eventual proliferation of automobiles. French architect **Jacques Gréber**, brought in by Prime Minister Mackenzie King to create the first real urban plan for the capital, suggested the creation of a greenbelt (which is the now 200-square-kilometre [125-sq-mi] space of protected wild and rural land surrounding the city) to help with the problems of natural growth, and the removal of the rail lines that crisscrossed the city during the first half of the century (you can still see remnants of old rail lines on Heron Road, for example, just west of Bank Street).

Located at Wellington Street and Rideau Canal, this was Ottawa's main passenger depot until 1966, when the city finally moved the station east, out of the downtown core, to the Walkley Road area. Despite the plans to demolish the building, the former station was renovated and opened a year later as the Canadian Government Conference Centre. Still used as a conference centre (remember the Meech Lake accord?), the building has also been a gallery (a section of rubble from the former Berlin Wall is on permanent display inside the main entrance), and had been considered as the location for the Canadian Sports Hall of Fame in the 1990s and a museum of Canadian political history (which has yet to be established) a few years later.

A new rail depot was built outside the downtown core to replace the existing one, and many of the rail lines were converted into controlled-access highways (including what eventually became the Transitway). All of this allowed for better automobile access to downtown, eliminated hazardous crossings, and created a series of paths for cyclists and pedestrians throughout the city. With Gréber's help, the electric streetcars were finally removed entirely in 1959. There have been rumours of bringing one back — perhaps along Sparks Street — but such a project has yet to be realized.

The Golden Age of Public Transport

Early public transportation began in Ottawa in 1866 with the launch of the **Ottawa City Passenger Railway Company**, with a horse-drawn tram running from New Edinburgh across town to the suspension bridge. The driver was expected to collect fares as well as drive, handing the reins off to passengers as fares were collected. By 1890, the **Ottawa Electric Street Railway Company** was operating electric streetcars, which were extremely popular. The first of their kind in Canada, these cars became known as the most modern in the country. The company started with only one line at first, from Broad Street station (now Centretown) to the Exhibition (now SuperEx), then extended the line farther to the Protestant Hospital at the corner of Charlotte and Rideau Streets, where it finally ended at the Canada Atlantic Station on Elgin Street. When the Ottawa City Passenger Railway Company requested permission to switch to electric trains so the company could compete, city council refused. Eventually, the two merged, and the Ottawa Electric Railway Company (minus the word "Street" in the name)

OCCUPATIONAL HAZARD

In 1906, a fire gutted the **Gilmour Hotel** on Bank Street. Three weeks after the blaze, Harry Lynch was driving Streetcar #22 along its scheduled route toward Gladstone Avenue when the Gilmour's remaining wall along Bank Street began to fall. Sensing imminent disaster, Lynch applied the brake but was unable to stop the car in time. Lynch, the conductor, and three passengers were seriously injured in the accident.

was formed in the summer of 1893. During the winter, sweeper units were used to keep tracks clear of snow. Early models of the electric trams, which left the crew open to harsh winter elements, were imported from Utica, New York around the turn of the century. Fortunately for operators, later models included an enclosed cabin to protect the driver from the -15°C (5°F) winter weather.

Last of the Steam Trains

Photo: Andrew Van Beek

Built in 1907, the **Hull-Chelsea-Wakefield Steam Train** is one of the country's last remaining authentic steam-powered trains, puffing its way south from the village of Wakefield to Gatineau, just over 60 kilometres (37 mi) away. The journey takes about half a day as it travels along the Gatineau River, through the Gatineau Park. Unfortunately, no one has figured out a way to get the train to run from Ottawa to Wakefield, but city folk can travel in steam-train style to the infamous music venue the **Black Sheep Inn** (see p. 126) for concerts and shows.

Adult fare for a return trip is $41 (May to mid-September) or $47 (mid-September to mid-October) during their scenic "Fall Foliage" season; discounted rates are available for seniors, students, and families, and children under two ride free. The company also offers a variety of packages for special tours and dinner and brunch trains.

165 rue Deveault (off rue de la Carrière), Gatineau, Quebec, 819-778-7246, steamtrain.ca

ROAD RAGE

According to the **Ontario's Worst Roads** website *(worstroads.ca)*, the trouble spot to avoid in Ottawa (if you can) is Limebank Road along River Road because of its high volume of traffic and its twists, turns, bumps, and almost nonexistent shoulder. All of this makes it very unsafe for biking as well.

According to the **City of Ottawa Road Safety** website, the worst accident spots for 2006 were Heron Road and Riverside Drive, King Edward Avenue and St. Patrick Street, and Baseline Road and Woodroffe Avenue, which together were the locations of over 100 automobile collisions.

GIDDYUP

Believe it or not, there are horse stables in the Byward Market. If you think about it, this isn't really a stretch, considering that **George and York Streets** were built twice as wide as normal in the 1800s to allow for horse-drawn carts, and there are even some interior courtyards in the neighbourhood that were expanded to allow carts to turn around after making deliveries. With the red barn and Belgian horses, as well as miniature ponies, hidden in the back of York Street for more than a couple of generations, **Cundell John Stables** at 113 York Street *(beside the Tea Party; 241-8054)* offers carriage, wagon, and winter sleigh rides. They also show horses at various country fairs throughout the Ottawa Valley.

TRAFFIC MONITORING

Ottawa has one of the largest and most sophisticated traffic-monitoring systems in North America, which sets the timing of traffic signals and adjusts for high-volume traffic or construction. At the **Traffic Control Centre**, video images are captured and collected every six seconds and displayed in real time — you can check out the images online at webcam.city.ottawa.on.ca/trafficvideo/video_en.htm. Situated in a City of Ottawa building on Gladstone Avenue, just a little west of Preston Avenue (175 Loretta Ave. N.), the centre sells decommissioned Ottawa street signs to the public for $10 each, from an online list of ones available including streets renamed after amalgamation (to avoid duplication), as well as those replaced for normal maintenance reasons.

GLEBE-HEAVY TRAFFIC

Originated in the late 1960s and early 70s by Glebe resident John Leaning and former mayor Charlotte Whitton, the **Traffic Plan** restricted — pay attention now — Carling Avenue to Bronson, renaming it Glebe Avenue within the Glebe, and stopping O'Connor Street at Isabella to route traffic around and not through the Glebe area, making the Glebe practically an urban island in the city. A second scheme, called the Centretown Plan, stemmed from this idea, and resulted in the restoration of the 1912 Pretoria Lift Bridge.

Whatever Floats Your Boat

Photo: Charles Earl

Lumber magnate Philemon Wright, realizing the need for passenger ships on the Ottawa River, built *The Packet* steam boat in 1819. It served the river from Wrightstown (or Wrightsville, then Hull) to Grenville at the head of the Long Sault Rapids. *The Packet* was subsequently replaced by larger, more efficient steam-powered vessels (all of which are now long gone), including the *Albert*, the *Empress*, and the *Victoria*. By the early 1870s, American boaters were plying the Rideau Canal in a variety of pleasure craft, but in those days, no boat was allowed into the canal system without flying the Union Jack — and lockmasters pocketed a good bit of extra cash selling flags to those wishing to enter Canadian waters. By the turn of the century, the pleasure boaters encouraged the establishment of several hotels, where travellers could dock their boats and obtain food and lodging, and bed-and-breakfasts gave way to clusters of cottages and camps along the Rideau waterway. These days, the waterway is littered with spots to dock your boat (if you have one), from **Dows Lake Pavilion** (1001 Queen Elizabeth Dr., 232-1001, dowslake.com) all the way south to **Rideau Acres Campground** (1014 Cunningham Rd., 546-2711, rideauacres.com), just north of Kingston, Ontario. Otherwise, for riverboat tours along the Ottawa River, check out either **Paul's Boat Lines** (225-6781, paulsboatcruises.com), departing from both the Ottawa Locks at their base between Parliament Hill and the Château Laurier on the Ontario side, or on the Quebec side at Hull Marina, located beside the Museum of Civilization and the Interprovincial Bridge. Alternatively, hire the *Ottawa River Queen* (an early 19th-century steam-powered paddle-wheeler) or *Miss Gatineau* for a private charter cruise from the **Ottawa Boat Cruise Company** (724-8408, ottawaboatcruise.com); the boats leave from the Quai des Artistes at the confluence of the Gatineau and Ottawa Rivers, under the Lady Aberdeen Bridge (Boul. Fournier).

Roads Most Traveled

King Edward Drive

One of the first projects completed by the Ottawa Improvement Commission (created by Prime Minister Wilfred Laurier in 1899), King Edward Drive was proposed as an alternative route to the muddy trail that connected Rideau Hall with Parliament Hill. The original trail was so bad that Viscount Monck (Sir Charles Stanley Monck, Canada's first Governor General) preferred to commute by boat rather than traverse the rugged distance on land. Landscape architect Frederick Todd pointed out that using the suggested half-mile portion of Rideau Street – with its horse-drawn streetcar tracks and heavy traffic – made the proposed alternate route unsuitable. Instead, Todd envisioned a stately drive along the top of the limestone cliffs on the south shore of the Ottawa River for use as the principal thoroughfare.

Richmond Road

This route could be considered the premier monument to earliest European activity in the Westboro neighbourhood. The autumn of 1818 saw the arrival of 400 soldiers (the bulk of whom were Irish immigrants) and their families in Westboro from Quebec at what became known as **Richmond Landing** (previously known as Bellows Landing, see p. 18), just behind Chaudière Falls, to build a main road which would be named for Charles Lennon, the fourth Duke of Richmond and Governor General of British North America who died in 1819 (after contracting rabies from a fox!). The entire group worked its way west along what became the Richmond Trail to arrive at their land grants, and settled their village beside the Jock River through a policy of assisted emigration. Unfortunately for the original Richmond Landing site, the National Capital Commission (NCC) in the early 1970s made a number of unpopular decisions ostensibly to improve Ottawa life, including pressing for the construction of the Portage Bridge, from Wellington Street across the water to Boulevard Maisonneuve, thus obliterating a significant portion of one of Ottawa's earliest heritage sites. (One of the few then-popular decisions the NCC made was to open up and maintain the Rideau Canal as an annual skating rink).

WHAT'S IN A NAME?

As the capital of a new Dominion, overrun by colonial industry and military, Ottawa was filled with streets named for statesmen, military officials, settlers and explorers, and early mayors. Some that lent their names included the Marquess of Wellington, the great English general, victor in the Peninsula and at Waterloo against Napoleon (Wellington St.); the Duke of Sussex, sixth son of George III (Sussex Dr., formerly Sussex St. – it was once known as Metcalf St. from Bolton St. to the Rideau; east of the Rideau it was called Ottawa St.); the eighth Earl of Elgin, Governor General of British North America (Elgin St.); the 12th Earl of Somerset, First Lord of the Admiralty (Somerset St.); the Marquess of Lorne, ninth Duke of Argyll, Governor General of Canada (Argyll St.); the Duke of Cumberland (Cumberland St.); Frederick Temple Blackwood, Marquess of Dufferin and Ava, Governor General of Canada (Dufferin Rd.); Lord Stanley of Preston, Governor General of Canada (Stanley Ave., once Rideau Rd.); and Baron Lisgar, Governor General of Canada (Lisgar St.).

Other roadway notables are fellow Bytown pioneers Nicholas Sparks (Sparks St.) and Daniel O'Connor, Treasurer of Carleton County (O'Connor St.), both of whom hoped that the cross-like symbol of their streets' intersection would help cool the conflicts between the town's Orange and Green factions; Henry Franklin Bronson, who operated a lumber mill at Chaudière Falls (Bronson Ave.); Allan Gilmour, a pioneering timber and lumber merchant (Gilmour St.); Sir George Etienne Cartier, Canadian statesman (Cartier St.); James Maclaren, active in lumbering in the region (Maclaren St.); British Statesman Anthony Ashley Cooper (Cooper St.); Sir Dominick Daly, Provincial Secretary for Lower Canada (Daly St.); Major Daniel Bolton, Royal Engineers, and the resident engineer officer for many years (Bolton St.); Joseph-Eugène-Bruno Guigues, the first Roman Catholic bishop of Ottawa (Guigues St.); and one must not forget Thomas Fuller, architect of the first Parliament Building (Fuller St.).

Dalhousie Street

This strange mixture of shops, apartment buildings, and heavy traffic, now one of Lowertown's main thoroughfares, is named for **George Ramsay**, the ninth Earl of Dalhousie, who was a driving force behind the building of the Rideau Canal. Dalhousie toured the Ottawa area in the summer of 1820 to look over the proposed site of the canal. He purchased the narrow 600-acre plot of land between the Ottawa River and Wellington Street, bordered on the west by Bronson and east by Rideau. Today the area includes not only Dalhousie Street, but Library and Archives Canada, the Supreme Court, the Parliament Buildings, the Rideau Centre, and the Byward Market.

Montreal Road

Lumber baron Philemon Wright did most of his local commuting east and west by way of the Ottawa River and found that he needed a more stable land route. A local Aboriginal man who was familiar with the geography offered to guide Wright and his party to their destination; their route eventually became Montreal Road, which was literally the road they used to get to Montreal.

Carling Avenue

This road is named for Sir John Carling, the one-time federal minister of agriculture who in the late 1800s established the first Dominion Experimental Farm. Originally well outside the city, the farm now resides between the modern-day Carling Avenue and Baseline Road.

Unbreakable Bridge

Completed in December 1827, the original Sappers Bridge linked Uppertown with Lowertown over the section of the Rideau Canal known as **Deep Cut**. The bridge was so well built that when it had to be demolished in 1912 to make way for Union Station, they couldn't actually break the structure apart, even with dynamite. The demolition crew finally had to drop a two-ton weight from a height of 50 feet several times in order to destroy the structure. Three years later, two of the stones from the original structure were used to mark the spot in

Major's Hill Park where the house owned by Colonel By (who built the Rideau Canal and for whom Bytown was named; see p. 29) had stood.

Taxi Bureaucracy

There are a pile of cab companies in the city, but the ones to be recommended in Ottawa are **Blue Line Taxi** (238-1111), **Capital Taxi** (744-3333) or **West-Way Taxi** (727-0101), and in Gatineau, **Royal Taxi** (819-777-5231). Because of the close proximity of our sister city across the river, located in another province, cabs from either cities can cross the bridge to deliver a passenger, but are not allowed to pick up a new passenger on their way back (which can lead to frustration when you see the wrong one going by, headed back to its home city for a fare, where you'd like to go). Still, the cab drivers in town are, for the most part, pretty friendly, and you might just get Ottawa poet and musician Bill Hawkins behind the wheel (see p. 81).

Cycle Paths

If you're sick to death of driving cars or hailing cabs, Ottawa is home to a number of lovely bike paths, many of which are also used for in-line skating. An extremely good and detailed map of Ottawa paths can be found at *bikedump.com/bikepath.html*, and for a list of current laws, parking, safety, clubs, tours, and rental information, you can check out *ottawakiosk.com/bike_guide.html*

If you don't have a bike of your own, you can always hire one at **Rent-A-Bike**, East Arch, Plaza Bridge, at the

OUT WITH THE OLD ...

It's about time a government town started using words like "efficient" and "cost-effective" when discussing results. In August 2007, Ottawa made history when a 216-wheel, self-propelled modular transporter helped to replace a 650-tonne westbound section of the **Island Park Bridge** (the main east-west highway that cuts through the city) also known as the Queensway. With a round-the-clock crowd of spectators, the engineering feat marked the first time a Canadian highway bridge replacement was undertaken using rapid-replacement technology, removing and installing the new section in less than 18 hours on the weekend to keep weekday commuter traffic moving. Previous technology would have shut down the highway for at least two years.

corner of Rideau and Colonel By Drive on the Canal (241-4140, rentabike.ca) or **Cyco's**, 5 Hawthorne Avenue (567-8180, cycosport.ca).

Up, Up, and Away

If you've ever flown in or out of the **Ottawa Macdonald-Cartier International Airport** (named for Sirs John A. Macdonald and George-Etienne Cartier) over the past few years, you will have noticed the impressive new structure, the Ottawa airport passenger terminal building that opened in October 2003. Built with the "traveller's ease and comfort in mind," its open-space concept and waterfalls greet visitors as they arrive, making one feel much more like one is arriving in a world class city and not a cultural backwater. Originally opened at Uplands (before Ottawa had moved that far south) by the Ottawa Flying Club in 1928 (which still operates from there), the site hosted the No. 2 Service Flying Training School during World War II, providing advanced pilot training in Harvard and Yale aircraft for the British Commonwealth Air Training Plan. Ottawa's airport, a mere 10 kilometres (6 mi) south of the city centre, is easy to access through local bus transit (or take the YOW Shuttle Service to and from the airport to any downtown hotel) (260-2359, yowshuttle.com). In March 2006, it was named the second best airport in the Americas (with Halifax International Airport coming in first) and among the 10 best worldwide by Airports Council International. ottawa-airport.ca

Air Alternatives

If you have other airport needs (whatever they could be), or just like to watch cloud busters, you can always check out the small commercial **Carp Airport** (1500 Thomas Argue Rd., 839-5276, cyrp.ca) situated in the west end of the Capital Region, the **Gatineau-Ottawa Executive Airport** (819-663-0737, 1700, rue Arthur-Fecteau, ville.gatineau.qc.ca/dev-econ/aeroport-ang .htm) just across the Ottawa River, or the **Embrun Airport** (443-1341) to the east.

Photo: Olga Novoa

Given all the Ottawa greenery (including the 200-sq-km space
of protected wild and rural land that surrounds the city), it's no wonder
we love the outdoors. Recognized as one of the most well-treed cities
in Canada, Ottawa is practically as rural as it is urban. And with
a plethora of year-round outdoor sporting events, not only do we embrace
the cold weather in winter, we revel in it.

The Birthplace of Lord Stanley's Mug

It's appropriate that the **Stanley Cup**, the ultimate trophy awarded for our "national game," originated in the nation's capital. In 1892, at a dinner of the Ottawa Amateur Athletic Association, Lord Kilcoursie, a player on the **Ottawa Rebels** hockey club, delivered a message on behalf of Lord Frederick Stanley, Governor General of Canada, announcing the awarding of a trophy to the best team in Canadian hockey. (Unfortunately, since Lord Stanley returned to his native England in the midst of the 1893 season, he never witnessed a championship game nor attended a presentation of the trophy.) There's a plaque in front of a laundromat at Gladstone Avenue and Percy Streets, the former site of **Patinoire Dey's Skating Rink**, where one of the first games for the cup was played, and where the **Ottawa Senators** (popularly known as "the silver seven") defeated the Montreal Victorias on March 10, 1903 to give Ottawa its first Cup title. Today, the Stanley Cup is the oldest trophy that can be won by a professional sports team in North America.

No Respect

Hockey's most hallowed prized has suffered much abuse and misuse over the years – some of it involving Ottawa teams. In 1903, a member of the Cup-winning **Ottawa Senators** (the "Silver Seven") decided to take the trophy home with him. When a teammate found out, a fight ensued, which somehow led to the Cup being tossed into a cemetery. Another odd event occurred two years later when the Silver Seven won it again. One of the drunken celebrants boasted he could kick the Cup across the frozen Rideau Canal (remember, this was when the Cup wasn't much larger than a soup bowl, and rugby was a more popular sport in the Ottawa Valley). Not surprisingly, the Cup didn't make it across the canal, and somehow got left behind as the party moved elsewhere. Fortunately, when the team returned the next morning, they found the Cup sitting on top of the ice, right where they had left it. A subsequent win by the same team in 1927 led to the Cup being left in King Clancy's living room, where he ended up using it to hold items like letters, bills, chewing gum, and cigar butts. Fortunately (or unfortunately, if you like these sorts of stories), a representative of the Hockey Hall of Fame now accompanies the Stanley Cup wherever it goes so such incidents can be avoided in the future.

Go, Sens, Go!

Photo: John W. MacDonald

In 1989, Ottawa real estate developer Bruce Firestone launched his bid to revive the **Ottawa Senators**, a National Hockey League team that had been defunct since 1934. Firestone brought in Frank Finnigan – the last surviving member of the 1927 Stanley Cup-winning Senators – as the bid's public face. The bid was a success and in 1992, Ottawa had its team back. But by 1993, new owner Rod Bryden was already struggling to keep the team alive, though he managed to borrow $188 million

During the 2004 NHL strike, Ottawa businesswoman and nationally known sex expert Sue McGarvie spiced things up from the then-new location of her Love and Romance store – not far from the hockey arena in Kanata – with lingerie ads that said, "Why they're still making passes in Kanata," and "The only place to score in Kanata this season." Under new ownership, the store still exists in three Ottawa locations as the **Couples Love and Romance Store** (1489E Merivale Rd., 727-5534) and as the **Couples Romance Stores** (F-876 Montreal Rd., 744-0540 and 1473 Richmond Rd., 820-6032).

TROUBLED WATERS

In June 2007, a scheduled show by former Pink Floyd front man **Roger Waters** at Scotiabank Place was bumped four days to make room for an Ottawa Senators playoff game. How's that for hockey devotion?

LEAFS VS. SENS

You can always tell an old bar from a new one by the team it promotes. The venerable **Carleton Tavern**, for example, is still very much a Toronto Maple Leafs bar despite the NHL's return to Ottawa in 1992. Many other watering holes around the city, though, sport logos, banners, and flags for the "Sens."

for the Senators' arena, the Palladium, since renamed the Corel Centre, and then **Scotiabank Place** *(1000 Palladium Dr., 599-0100)*, and even built off-ramps from the highway to ease arena access. Making the playoffs (or at least getting pretty close) each year, the revived Ottawa Senators are usually one of the best teams in the Eastern Conference, but to date they still haven't managed to win back the Cup they first won in 1903. *ottawasenators.com*

The Senior Senators

The original Ottawa Senators were one of the NHL's strongest teams from 1918 to 1927, capturing the Stanley Cup four times during this period. They were part of the original NHL, launched in 1917, before the team folded in 1934. These Senators boasted future Hall of Famers Clint Benedict (goalie), Harry "Punch" Broadbent (right wing), Cy Denneny (left wing), and Frank "Dutch" Nighbor (centre).

Hockey Night in Ottawa

Organized hockey in Ottawa arguably originated in 1890, when the Ontario Hockey Association was formed, and the Ottawa team (they were known simply as that at the time) became the first OHA champions. In 1903, the Ottawa Senators won the Stanley Cup, the first of 10 times (so far) that the trophy was awarded to an Ottawa team. For many years, hockey was played at the auditorium at the corner of O'Connor and Argyle, which opened at the start of the 1923–24 ice hockey season, but closed in 1967, to be sold to the YMCA-YWCA as the site for their new high-rise building.

The Captain

When the Ottawa Senators returned to the NHL in 1992, the franchise retired the number eight, which was the number of **Frank Finnigan**, captain of the original Senators and a local boy from Shawville, a village in Pontiac County across the river in Quebec. Unfortunately, since Finnigan had died the year before, he not only didn't see his number retired (the first and so far only one the team has thus honoured), he never saw the resurgence of the franchise. There's a restaurant named Frank Finnigan's in Scotiabank Place, festooned with photographs and memorabilia.

Photo: Lois Siegel

AND THE KIDS ARE ALRIGHT
Ottawa's junior hockey team, **The Ottawa 67's** *(ottawa67s. com)*, have been part of the Ontario Hockey League since they started in 1967, Canada's centennial year, filling the void left by the Ottawa Junior Canadiens and the Hull-Ottawa Canadiens, two teams that folded in 1963. The 67's have appeared in the Memorial Cup tournament five times, winning twice. They have also won the J. Ross Robertson Cup three times, the Hamilton Spectator Trophy three times, and have won 12 division titles. Across the river, you can also check out **Les Gatineau Olympiques** (formerly the Hull Festivals; *lesolympiques.net)* at the Robert Guertin Centre.

The King

Perhaps the most famous hockey player to emerge from the Ottawa region is **Francis Michael "King" Clancy**. As a youth, his original skates were hand-me-downs from Senators winger Eddie Gerard – a friend of Clancy's father – and when King joined the Senators himself in 1921, not only was Gerard a teammate, but Clancy was still wearing his colleague's old skates. Clancy debuted as the youngest player in the NHL to date (17 years old). He was a key contributor to the Senators' 1927 Stanley Cup win – the team's 10th Cup victory. In 1930, he was traded to the Toronto Maple Leafs, where he played out the rest of his Hall of Fame career. Aside from some forays into coaching in Montreal, Clancy remained chiefly associated with the Toronto Maple Leafs for the rest of his life, as coach, and later, as an assistant to the team's general manager.

Sens Mile

On May 19, 2007, the Ottawa Senators beat the Buffalo Sabres in game four of the eastern conference, thus putting the Senators in the Stanley Cup finals for the first time since 1927. Minutes after the overtime game-winning goal by team captain Daniel Alfredsson – "Alfie" to locals – thousands of Ottawa fans immediately rushed outside to baptize what is now known as the "Sens Mile," an Elgin Street fan zone similar to Calgary's "Red Mile" or Edmonton's Whyte Avenue. Originally waffling over the idea of the designation, Mayor Larry O'Brien speculated he would allow such a thing if (not *when*, I might add) the Ottawa Senators made it into the Stanley Cup finals. Thankfully, even with an estimated crowd of some 8,000 people (somewhat inebriated and loud, but otherwise polite), there were only three arrests by 10 p.m. that night: one for assault, one for public intoxication, and another for breach of probation. You have to appreciate how so many people actually caused so few problems. I guess it helps, too, that the city

Photo: John W. MacDonald

FOR THOSE WHO LIKE TO WATCH

The most important part of any sporting event – whether it be an Ottawa Senators playoff game or **Monday Night Football** –

is having a good place to watch it. Here are some recommendations:

Boston Pizza: 2980 Conroy Rd., 248-0802, bostonpizza.com

Broadway Bar & Grill: 1896 Prince of Wales Dr., 224-7004, broadwaybarandgrill.com

Buffalo Charlie's Bar & Grill: 2525 Carling Ave., 828-8988, buffalocharlies.com

The Carleton Tavern: 223 Armstrong St. at Parkdale, 728-4424

Don Cherry's Sports Grill: 290 Rideau St., 241-9150, doncherrys.com

police have so much experience with crowd control after years of shepherding tens of thousands of people along Parliament Hill every Canada Day.

Bad Fans, Good Fans

An unfortunate offshoot of "us" is "them," and in May 2007, some visiting Buffalo Sabres fans saw the worst of us when Buffalo resident **Renee Luck** was attacked post-game in Ottawa by Senators fans during the Eastern Conference finals. However, it should be pointed out that she was rescued by *other* Senators fans. The Ottawa franchise quickly offered free tickets, travel, and accommodation to Luck after hearing about the incident, and hopefully her first visit to Ottawa won't be the last.

A-Skating We Will Go

Officially the world's longest outdoor skating rink, the **Rideau Canal** stretches 7.8 kilometres (4.8 mi) of "skateway" from downtown Ottawa to Dow's Lake near Carleton University – roughly the equivalent of 100 hockey rinks end-to-end. Skating on the canal remains one of the key elements of the **Winterlude** festival (see p. 157) in February of every year, despite the fact that the changing temperatures have been shortening the skating season over the past few winters. During Winterlude, various points along the canal include heated shelters, rest areas, change rooms, skate rentals, washrooms, picnic tables, and fire pits, as well as almost 40 sets of stairs along its length.

Another place for free skating is the outdoor rink in front of **Ben Franklin Place** at 101 Centrepointe Drive (no hockey sticks, strollers, or human chains allowed on the ice). If skating on the canal freaks you out (though it shouldn't), there's always the historic **Minto Skating Club** *(733-5292)* and **Minto Skating Centre** *(ice rental, 733-7800)* at 2571 Lancaster Road, where many an Olympian got her start (including figure skaters Barbara Ann Scott and Lynn Nightingale).

Photo: Charles Earl

Skating Sweetheart

The preeminent figure in the history of skating in Ottawa is Olympian **Barbara Ann Scott**. Known as "Canada's Sweetheart," Scott was the first Canadian to win Olympic figure skating gold at the 1948 Winter Games in St Moritz, Switzerland. She was also the first citizen of a non-European nation to win a world figure skating championship. And if that weren't enough, the Reliable Toy Company created a Barbara Ann Scott doll to honour her Olympic accomplishments.

Photo: John W. MacDonald

When she retired from skating, Scott turned to equestrian competition. She was inducted into Canada's Sports Hall of Fame in 1955, the American Sports Hall of Fame in 1980 (as North American skating champion) and into the International Sports Hall of Fame in 1997.

Yousuf Karsh portrait of Barbara Ann Scott

BUMP, SET, SPIKE!
The annual **Hope Volleyball Tournament** *(hopehelps.com/ ottawa_home.cfm)* takes place on Mooney's Bay Beach in July; it raises money for local charities and features a lot of cool bands.

A Feel for Skating

You don't necessarily need to see where you're going – or hear, for that matter – to be a speed skating champion. This may sound unbelievable, but in the case of **Kevin Frost**, a resident of Ottawa suburb Orléans, it's true. Unfortunately, though, the International Paralympic Committee doesn't recognize **deaf-blind speed skating** as a sport. Frost suffers from Usher Syndrome, a rare genetic disorder that causes progressive hearing and vision loss; Frost's sight has been reduced to tunnel vision at eight percent of normal visual range, and he's only able to hear sounds that register at 90 decibels (imagine heavy traffic or a noisy home appliance) or above. Still, he managed to graduate from Gloucester High School with the help of a hearing aid and learning to lip-read. On top of it all, he won two silver and two bronze medals in his rookie year of competitive speed skating. He has been petitioning for years to get his category accepted as a Paralympic sport. Check out *deafblindspeedskater.com*

CHECKING CONDITIONS

If you're looking for current ski or skate conditions, the **National Capital Commission** offers information lines: **Gatineau Park Information and Ski Conditions** at 819-827-2020 or 1-800-465-1867, and **Rideau Canal Skateway Conditions** at 239-5234.

Hit the Slopes

Lord Frederick Hamilton introduced skiing to the Ottawa area in 1887. Brother-in-law of Lord Lansdowne, Governor General, Hamilton brought a pair of Russian skis with him during his stay at Rideau Hall. Though his first skiing demonstrations were booed by some onlookers (not all new ideas are greeted with open arms), the activity soon caught on.

By the late 1930s, when the popularity of the sport soared, roughly a third of the 50,000 skiers in Ontario lived in Ottawa. Once considered one of the great skiing centres of this continent and the world, Ottawa is now home to the **Canadian Ski Museum** at 200-1960 Scott Street, where you can find a detailed history of skiing, and a collection of old skis and ski equipment from Canada and around the world *(open daily, closed holidays; 722-3584, skimuseum.ca)*.

Image from the Paul Roy Gift, prepared by David Three Rats

All in the Family

Ottawa's **Anne Heggtveit** won the 1960 Winter Olympics gold medal in slalom at Squaw Valley, California. Heggtveit, whose father, Halvor, was a Canadian cross-country champion, first gained acclaim when she became, at 15 years of age, the youngest winner ever of the Holmenkollen Giant Slalom competition in Norway in 1954. In addition to winning Canada's first-ever Olympic skiing gold, she was also the first non-European to win the International Ski Federation slalom and overall world championship. She was inducted into Canada's Sports Hall of Fame in 1960, and has a ski run named after her at Camp Fortune Ski Resort.

Gone But Not Forgotten

Ottawa has a reputation in the sports world as a place where franchises come and go. The Ottawa Senators are a good example – but hopefully they'll stick around this time. Here are a few notable teams that have disappeared. For now. . . .

The (Former) Rough Riders

The Canadian Football League has never included more than a dozen teams at a time. Why is it, then, that for years there were *two* teams with the same name: the Ottawa Rough Riders and the still-functioning Saskatchewan Roughriders? (Note word-spacing difference to avoid confusion.) Founded as the Ottawa Football Club in 1876, the Rough Riders folded in 1996, plagued by poor attendance and general mismanagement during its last few years. More nomenclature confusion: the team was briefly known as the Ottawa Senators during the 1920s (after the demise of the original hockey team) before taking the name the Rough Riders. One story claims the name has its origins

FORTUNE-ATELY

Ottawa's best option for a winter ski vacation is **Camp Fortune** (campfortune.com), only a 15-minute drive from downtown. It boasts 20 ski trails, ranging from beginner to experienced. During the off-season it has great mountain biking trails.

Two other options would be **Mont Cascades** (448 Mont Cascades Rd., 888-282-2722, montcascades.ca) in nearby Cantley, Quebec, with night-skiing, snowboarding, and 19 trails; or **Mont Tremblant** in Mont Tremblant, Quebec (819-425-8681, tremblant.ca), a farther drive outside Ottawa (about two hours), but it has the highest peak in the Laurentian Mountains and plenty of other winter activities to keep you busy, including dogsledding, horseback riding, ice climbing, cross-country skiing, and a snow park (like a skate park, but for snowboarders), which includes an Olympic-sized half pipe.

Other Ski Locations in the Ottawa Area:

Calabogie Peaks Resort: Calabogie (near Arnprior), Ontario, 752-2720, calabogie.com

Edelweiss: Wakefield, Quebec, 819-459-2328, mssi.ca/en/edelweiss

Mont Ste. Marie: Mont Ste. Marie, Quebec, 819-467-5200, montstemarie.com

Mount Pakenham: Pakenham, Ontario, 624-5290, mountpakenham.com

Vorlage: Wakefield, Quebec, 819-459-2301, skivorlage.com

Photo: Lois Siegel

BATTER UP

Ottawa may be a hockey town, but it's also home to a little factory that just happens to produce bats for Major League Baseball's all-time home run king. Barry Bonds and a number of other major leaguers use bats produced by the **Original Maple Bat Corporation**, founded by Ottawa's Sam Holman, who produces well over 10,000 bats a year in his inconspicuous shop. Developed in 1997, the "Sam Bat" is made out of Canadian maple; it doesn't dent easily and thus lasts longer than any others.

Holman claims that living in Ottawa offered an advantage for developing his product. As the company's website says: "[Ottawa] was a researcher's dream centre: home of the Canadian patent library, two first-rate universities, the Wood Council, the Canadian Forest Research Centre, the National and other extensive Libraries — all in the centre of the richest deciduous forest in North America."

in logging. Another says it's linked to Teddy Roosevelt's regiment of "Rough Riders" in the Spanish-American War. Yet another story credits the name to a Hamilton sports writer who used the words to describe the conduct of the Ottawa team during a match in 1898 against the Hamilton Tigers. Regardless, the team's glory years were during the 1960s and 70s, under the leadership of coach and general manager **Frank Clair**, who led the team to five Grey Cup titles.

The (Former) Renegades

Formed in 2002, the **Ottawa Renegades** returned football to Ottawa (briefly). In May 2005, Bernie Glieberman (who owned the Rough Riders) took ownership, naming his son Lonie team president. Occasionally, Lonie made newspaper headlines by pulling some boneheaded stunt or having some clever idea that never quite worked out, including an infamous Mardi Gras promotion that required women to bare their breasts (at what was ostensibly a family event) in exchange for coloured beads. A good enough team, the Renegades never got near the playoffs before being mothballed in April 2006. The team roster was divvied up among the remaining eight CFL teams in a draft. The late Renegades played in Frank Clair Stadium, named for the infamous Rough Riders coach and general manager.

Photo: Lois Siegel

The (Former) Lynx

Ottawa's own minor league baseball team, the **Lynx** were formed in 1993, and were for many years the farm team for the Montreal Expos (which *also* no longer exist). The Lynx were sold in August 2006, making them a Philadelphia Phillies affiliate. Even though they will continue to play out the 2007 season in Ottawa at **Lynx Stadium** *(300 Coventry Rd.)*, the team will be moved to Allentown, Pennsylvania, for the 2008 season, making them the Lehigh Valley IronPigs. Notable Lynx alumni include Orlando Cabrera, Ugueth Urbina, Javier Vazquez, José Vidro, and Canadian Adam Loewen.

Hall of Legends

For further information on Ottawa sporting legends, be sure to check out the **Ottawa Sports Hall of Fame** *(ottawasportshalloffame.com)* on the second level concourse at Scotiabank Place. Founded in 1966, the Hall is open whenever Scotiabank Place is, and has since inducted more than 200 members, including Cyclone Taylor, Larry Robinson, Denis Potvin, Aurel Joliat, Mark Kosmos, Phil Maloney, Franklin Thomas Ahearn, Francis (Frank) Amyot, Marjorie Blackwood, Donald Booth, Sheryl Boyle, Cyril Joseph (Cy) Denneny, Francois Xavier (Frank) Boucher, and John George (Buck) Boucher.

Dr Hoops

If you travel a bit west of town, between Almonte and the Mill of Kintail, you'll find a roadside plaque commemorating **Dr James Naismith**, the inventor of the game of basketball, who was born nearby. A physical education teacher and Presbyterian minister, he invented the game while working in Massachusetts in 1891.

A Local Mistake

A "Mulligan" is a golf term that refers to a "do-over," or free shot to substitute for a mistake. But who was the original "Mulligan," the lax linksman who gave the shot its name? Turns out it was **David Bernard Mulligan**, who during the 1920s ran the **Lord Elgin Hotel** on Elgin Street for a while before moving to the United States. Originally born in Pembroke, Ontario, Mulligan was a member of a number of clubs, including the St Lambert Country Club in Quebec. A real comedian, he *insisted* on repeating failed swings during his games, and for whatever reason, he not only got away with it, it also became a running joke.

YOUR MOVE

For board games and more, check out **Chess Talk** *(250 Bank St., 565 3662, chesstalk.com/boutique/store)*; if they don't have it, you simply don't need it. Poker players can check out **World Poker Depot** *(200 Laurier Ave. W. [inside NFNutrition], 859-7547, worldpokerdepot.com).*

ROLLIN', ROLLIN', ROLLIN'

Ottawa skaters Honey Bee and Liz Fox launched a local **roller derby** revival when they decided to start a team in 2007 to compete with existing squads in Montreal, Hamilton, Toronto, and London. Is Ottawa ready for women on skates crashing into each other? They currently get together every Saturday during summer at Brewer Arena in Old Ottawa South *(210 Hopewell Ave., 247-4917 myspace.com/ottawarollerderby)*; they also hold a roller disco in the same location a few times each summer.

SHALLOWER WATERS

If you don't want a full pool to splash around in, whether indoors or outdoors, you can always take your small child to one of Ottawa's **wading pools**. There are slew of them around the city (58, by last count). Lifeguards are situated at the larger pools, and a number of them are even attached to community centres that hold day-camp programs in the summer for kids. For a list of pools and their locations, follow the links at *ottawa.ca/residents/parks_recreation.*

In 2006, Ottawa pediatrician Kathy Keely took over as the first female president in the 115-year history of the **Royal Ottawa Golf Club** *(1405 Aylmer Rd., 819-777-3866, rogc.com)*. Female members were granted the same rights as men – including the right to vote and access to the president's lounge and parts of the clubhouse verandah – only 10 years earlier, ending a century of discrimination. The exclusive club was founded in 1891 during Queen Victoria's reign, and given its "royal" designation by King George V in 1912.

To take your own "Mulligans," you can either play here (check for availability) or at a whole slew of other golf courses in Ottawa and around Ottawa, including the **Eagle Creek Golf Course** *(109 Royal Troon La., Dunrobin, 832-3400)*, the **Marshes Golf Club at Brookstreet** *(320 Terry Fox Dr., 271-1800, brookstreet. ca/golf)*, the **Metcalfe Golf and Country Club** *(1956 8th Line Rd., Metcalfe, 821-3673, metcalfegolf.com)*, the **Pine View Municipal Golf Course** *(1471 Blair Rd., Gloucester, 746-4653, pineview.com)*, the **Rockcliffe Golf Driving Range** *(CFB Ottawa North, 746-4957)*, and the **Casselview Golf and Country Club** *(in Casselman, Hwy. 417 E.t, exit 66, about 25 minutes from Ottawa, 798-4653, casselview.com)*. For the much smaller version of the game, check out the **Game Professional Miniature Golf Course** *(3708 Navan Rd., 841-2323, thegamepmg.com)*, **Mini Golf Gardens** *(2 Collonade Rd. N., 723-5359, minigolfgardens.com)*, or **Capital Golf Centre** *(3798 Bank St., 521-2612, capitalgolf.ca)*.

An Alternative Triathalon

Called "The Ultimate Canadian Triathalon," the **Carleton Cup** combines skating, running, and drinking in an annual race down Rideau Canal to raise money for the Canadian Cystic Fibrosis Foundation. Started in 1989 as a diversion to make winter more tolerable for Carleton University students, the race traditionally takes place on the first Saturday of Winterlude. It starts at the Carleton University campus, moves down the Rideau Canal, and ends at a pub in the Byward Market. Far from helping Carleton University work against its reputation as a slacker school, the Carleton Cup has become a local tradition and even gained a bit of international attention (it didn't hurt that comedian Mike Myers once wore a Carleton Cup T-shirt while on *Saturday Night Live*). Kudos also came from such notable Canadian icons as Pierre Berton, Maurice "Rocket" Richard, and Stompin' Tom Connors. *carletoncup.ca*

Cues and Pins

There aren't a whole lot of options for pool in Ottawa, but there are enough. One of the classier places is **MacLaren's on Elgin** *(301 Elgin St., 236-2766, maclarens.com)*; with a hardwood décor and upscale menu, it also boasts 21 custom-made pool tables. If you prefer a pool hall with a bit more grit, like somewhere your father or grandfather might have played, check out **Cue 'N' Cushion Billiards & Bar** *(319 Bank St., 237-2404)*. If you're looking for something with a solid working-class environment (and cheaper beer), the **Orange Monkey** in the City Centre building *(250 City Centre Ave., 230-2850)* is the way to go. Other good options: **D Joint Pinball Billiards** *(411 McArthur Ave., 741-9177)* or the west end **Greenbank Broken Cue** *(250-A Greenbank Rd., 820-4889, brokencue.com)*.

If bowling is more your style, there are five-pin options at **Walkley Bowl** *(2092 Walkley Rd., 521-0132, walkleybowl.com)*, **Orleans Bowling Center** *(885 Taylor Creek Dr., 837-7000, orleansbowling.com)*, and **West Park Bowling Lanes** *(1205 Wellington St. W., 728-0933)*. For 10-pin, you have to go to the **McArthur Lanes** *(175 McArthur Rd., 745-2117, mcarthurlanes.com)*.

COME SAIL AWAY

The original site of the Britannia Aquatic Club, founded in 1887, was an old mill on Lac Deschênes. As the Britannia Boating Club, they had a number of teams in competitions, and won the Canadian War Canoe Championship in 1902, later won by the Ottawa Canoe Club in 1904; further, boat club member and Ottawa resident Frank Amyot won the gold medal in 1,000-metre (0.6-mi) paddling at the 1936 Berlin Olympics. Currently known as the **Britannia Yacht Club** *(828-5167, byc.ca)*, they have ample facilities for boating, sailing, and tennis, as well as a large banquet hall.

There were complaints about Ottawa city planner Jacques Gréber when he started creating a horseshoe of green space around Ottawa in the 1950s (frustrated developers called him "Jacques *Grabber*"). But thanks to him, we now have 200 square kilometres (124 sq mi) of greenbelt around the downtown core alone. For picnicking, swimming, Frisbee, hiking, snowshoeing – you name it – here are some locations worth considering (depending on your goals, of course). (Inline skaters can use the miles and miles of paths that line either side of the Rideau Canal, from Wellington Street/Rideau Street all the way down to Hog's Back, and back.)

Photo: France Rivet

POOL PARTY

There are a number of **public pools** around town, including many outdoor ones attached to community centres. They include: **Brewer Pool** *(100 Brewer Way, 247-4938)*, **Canterbury** *(2185 Arch St., 247-4865)*, **Champagne Pool** *(321 King Edward Ave., 244-4402)*, **Deborah Anne Kirwan Pool** *(1300 Kitchener Ave., 247-4820)*, **Dovercourt** *(411 Dovercourt Ave., 798-8951, x234)*, **Goulbourn Recreation Complex** *(1500 Shea Rd., 831-1169)*, **Jack Purcell Pool** *(320 Jack Purcell La., 564-1027)*, **Kanata Wave Pool & Leisure Centre** *(70 Aird Pl., 591-9283)*, **Lowertown Pool** *(40 Cobourg Str., 244-4406)*, **Nepean Sportsplex** *(1701 Woodroffe Ave., 580-2828)*, **Orléans Recreation Complex** *(1490 Youville Dr., 824-0819)*, **Pinecrest** *(2250 Torquay Ave., 828-3118)*, **Plant Bath** *(930 Somerset St. W., 232-3000)*, **Sawmill Creek** *(3380 D'Aoust Ave.)*, **Splash Wave Pool** *(2040 Ogilvie Rd., 748-4222)*, **St-Laurent** *(525 Côté St., 742-6767)*, and **Walter Baker Sports Centre** *(100 Malvern Dr., 580-2788)*.

Andrew Haydon Park, Acres Road and Carling Avenue: In the west end of the city, this park is named after a former mayor of the City of Nepean. It sits on the Ottawa River and has a view of Britannia Bay. Includes a picnic area, artificial lake, road concession, and yacht club. Considering the state of some parts of the Ottawa River, swimming is *not* recommended.

Commissioners Park (at Dow's Lake), Carling Avenue at Queen Elizabeth Driveway: Home to the **Dow's Lake Boathouse**, with concessions and restaurants, this is a popular spot during many regattas, as well as during the **Tulip Festival** in May, and the **Winterlude** carnival in February.

Confederation Park, Elgin Street at Laurier Avenue: Across the street from the new City Hall *(110 Laurier Ave. W.)*, this is the site of various events throughout the year, including **Winterlude**, the **Ottawa Jazz Festival**, and **Canada Day celebrations**, as well as many others. The fountain here once stood in Trafalgar Square in London, England.

Dow's Lake: Formerly Dow's Swamp, Dow's Lake was created during the construction of the Rideau Canal, and its proximity to Confederation Park, the Central Experimental Farm, and Dow's Lake Boathouse make it a good spot for picnickers and boat enthusiasts.

Garden of the Provinces, Wellington at Bay Streets: Across from the Library and Archives Canada building, this park commemorates the union of 10 provinces and the territories with flags, bronze plaques featuring the provincial flowers, and a symbolic fountain overlooking LeBreton Flats and the start of the Ottawa River Parkway.

Gatineau Park *(canadascapital.gc.ca/gatineau)*: a 15-minute drive north of downtown Ottawa, this park is home to a whole slew of trails for biking, walking, snowshoeing, skiing, or hiking.

Photo: France Rivet

Hog's Back Falls (officially known as Prince of Wales Falls), Hog's Back Road at Colonel By Drive: Near Carleton University, these falls are where the Rideau Canal passes through the first locks in Ottawa, with a swing bridge to enable sailing boats to pass under the roadway. Hog's Back Park and nearby Vincent Massey Park are both popular spots.

Jacques Cartier Park, Rue Laurier, Gatineau: This park, situated between the Interprovincial and Macdonald-Cartier bridges, has great views of Rideau Falls and Nepean Point, and is a popular festival events location, with the Outaouais Tourism office nearby, and the Canadian Museum of Civilization across the street. Pathways connect to Leamy Lake and the Gatineau River.

Leamy Lake Ecological Park and Archaeological Site, Leamy Lake Parkway, accessed from Boulevard Maissoneuve, Gatineau: Where the Gatineau River meets the Ottawa River, this was once a stopping-off

LIFE'S A BEACH

If you feel safer with lifeguard supervision while you're out in the sand, here are some beaches the City keeps an eye on: **Britannia Beach** *(2805 Carling Ave., 820-1211)*, **Mooney's Bay Beach** *(2926 Riverside Dr., 248-0863)*, and **Westboro Beach** *(follow Ottawa River Pkwy. to Kitchissippi Lookout)*.

point for the First Nations peoples as well as French fur traders, and has since been recognized as a rich site for archaeological digs. The park also has a lake with swimming and windsurfing, and a concession stand. The new Casino de Hull is directly across from Leamy Lake beach.

Photo: France Rivet

FOR THE BIRDS

One of the foremost birders in North America is Ottawa-born **Bruce Di Labio**, who currently lives just outside Ottawa in the village of Carp. A member of the **Ottawa Field-Naturalist's Club** (which is the oldest natural history club in Canada, dating back to 1879), Di Labio spent much of the 1980s working for the Museum of Nature in ornithology before working for the Canadian Nature Federation as Staff Naturalist and finally launching his own birding business in 1998. He conducts birding classes, field trips, and local group tours in Canada, and has also led birding tours to Arizona, Alaska, Texas, New Jersey, California, Costa Rica, Cuba, and Churchill, Manitoba. *www3.sympatico.ca/bruce.dilabio* (See also the Ottawa Field-Naturalists' Club website, *ofnc.ca*)

Major's Hill Park, Mackenzie Avenue (behind the Château Laurier Hotel): The city's oldest park, it was developed in 1874 for its view of the Parliament Buildings, and was once the home of Lieutenant-Colonel John By (though his home is long gone). Currently the park is the site of the Astrolabe Theatre and the noon gun, fired daily off Nepean Point.

Mer Bleue Conservation Area, Anderson Road off Inness Road: This parkland is a peat bog, more typical of what you might find in Canada's far north, despite being located southeast of the city.

New Edinburgh Park, Stanley Avenue and Dufferin Road: On the eastern bank of the Rideau River, this park has plenty of wildlife, including blue herons, muskrats, turtles, and butterflies. In the winter, there is an outdoor skating rink.

Pine Grove Forest, Hunt Club at Conroy Roads: This 12-square-kilometre (7.5-sq-mi) urban forest, managed by the National Capital Commission, combines natural and planted forest, and offers wide and level trails for hiking.

Vincent Massey Park, Heron Road (west of Riverside Dr., 733-7704): Just north of Hog's Back Park and Mooney's Bay, this park, named for Canada's first Canadian-born Governor General, is used for events involving large groups, with numerous picnic tables and fireplaces as well as softball fields, horseshoe pits, and a bandstand; in winter, it has some of the best tobogganing hills in the city. A parking fee of $4 is charged from May to October each year.

At one point, Ottawa was said to have more restaurants per capita than any other city in the country. Who says a government town is a bad thing? And being the nation's capital, our restaurants not only rate with some of the best in the world, but the range and quality of ethnic food options are spectacular. You just have to know where to look.

Thank God It's Friday's

Built in 1875 in a combination of French Modern and Italian styles, the building that now houses **Friday's Roast Beef House and Piano Parlour** was designed by Braddish Billings III (grandson of the original resident of what became Billings Bridge) and is one of the last structures along that strip of Elgin Street from the period. An Ottawa standard for over a quarter of a century, this restaurant has a Victorian atmosphere that blends upscale with just the right amount of casual; there's a good mixture of professional and government after-work types, and the kids who look barely old enough to shave. The menu features a wide range: sirloin, filet mignon, and rib eye steaks; lobster, shrimp, and scallops; duck, lamb, and prime rib. Be sure to check out their infamous desserts while you're there, too, including Friday's classic apple pie or the Victorian chocolate cake.
150 Elgin St., 237-5353

Eat Your Veggies

It seems you can't throw a stone in this town without hitting a vegetarian restaurant. One of the best has to be the **Roses Café** *(523 Gladstone Ave., 233-5574; 1285 Wellington St. W., 798-9191)*, which serves Indian food at its two locations. If Indian doesn't float your boat, you can always purchase a veggie meal by weight at either **The Green Door Restaurant** *(198 Main St., 234-9597, thegreendoor.ca)*, a favourite of hometown girl Alanis Morissette, or at the **Table Vegetarian Restaurant** *(1230 Wellington St. W., 729-5973, thetablerestaurant.com)*, which we *highly* recommend for its quality, range, and reasonable prices. Other meat-free highlights include **Govinda's Vegetarian Buffet** *(212 Somerset St. E., 565-6544)*, the **Peace Garden Café** *(47 Clarence St., 562-2434)*, **Perfection Satisfaction Promise** *(167 Laurier Ave. E., 234-7299, perfectionsatisfactionpromise.ca)*, and the **Pantry Vegetarian Tea Room** *(open 12 noon–3 p.m. only; 690 Lyon St., 233-2784)*, now over 30 years old, and quietly hidden at the back of the Glebe Community Centre.

The Mighty Oaks

Even if you're not a fan of restaurant chains, there's just something about the comfortable and classic British pub atmosphere of the **Royal Oak Pubs** that are sprinkled across Ottawa (10 locations in all; not including one that used to exist in Kingston). The original location, known as the **Bank Street Oak** (318 Bank St., 236-0190) is now three times the size of when it opened in 1980. Each pub has comfortable corners for individuals and groups, good quality pub fare, and a variety of activities including regular blues sessions (various locations). **The Laurier Oak** (161 Laurier Ave. E., 230-9223) hosts a series of literary readings (home to the Sasquatch Literary and Arts Performance Series, Tree Reading Series, and the BARD readings). The chain is named for the famed oak tree in England in which Charles II hid for a full day from Cromwell's army in 1651. The original Royal Oak location is but a shadow of its former self, but there are still an impressive number of other locations, with the more upscale at Bank and Gloucester Streets, the University of Ottawa version along Laurier Avenue East, or the Echo Drive Oak. Others include the **Downtown Oak** (188 Bank St., 232-1057), **Glebe Oak** (779 Bank St., 235-2624), **Gloucester Oak** (2067 Meadowbrook Rd., 741-0072), **Hunt Club Oak** (800 Hunt Club Rd. at Uplands, 248-1901), **Canal Oak** (221 Echo Dr., 234-3700), **Kanata Oak** (329 March Rd., 591-3895), **Orleans Oak** (1981 St Joseph Blvd., 834-9005), and **Wellington Oak** (1217 Wellington St., 728-6661) royaloakpubs.com

GRIST FOR THE GRISTMILL

The building that houses **The Mill** restaurant is just that – an old gristmill built in 1842. The quality of the food may not be what it used to be, but you can still watch the water flow through the mill wheel and imagine Ottawa as an old lumber town while drinking an expensive Chardonnay with the predominantly older, suit-and-tie set. Pope John Paul II stopped here to break bread in 1984 during his only tour of the capital. 555 Ottawa River Parkway (at Portage Bridge), 237-1311, the-mill.ca

Photo: John W. MacDonald

GREASY SPOONS

Whether it's late at night or early in the morning, and you're feeling hungry, head to **Mello's** *(290 Dalhousie St., 241-1909)* for good diner grub. It was a hangout for prostitutes before the "cleanup" in the late 1990s by the city pushed working women into less touristy parts of town. For some other good breakfasts, check **Ada's Diner** *(510 Bank St., 231-7959)* or **Al's Diner** *(834 Clyde Ave., 761-7488)*.

Pub Fare

Perhaps it's the Scottish Protestant in me, but I've always been a sucker for traditional pub fare. Here are a few options where you can get a good meal and a good pint: **Pickwick's Pub** *(422 MacKay St., 742-3169)*, the **Barley Mow** *(1060 Bank St., 730-1279, barleymow.com)*, Earl of Sussex Pub *(431 Sussex Dr., 562-5544)*, **Elephant & Castle Restaurant**, Rideau Centre *(corner of Rideau St. and Sussex Dr., 234-5544, elephantcastle.com)*, **New Edinburgh Pub** *(1 Beechwood Ave., 748-9809)*, **Patty's Pub**, which also features live Celtic music on occasion *(1186 Bank St., 730-2434)*, and **Pubwells** *(96 Preston St., 236-1175)*. For more standard pub food with a bit of a flair, go to the **Brig Pub** *(23 York St., 562-6666)*. Another Westboro choice we'd recommend would be **Wellington Gastropub** *(1325 Wellington St. W., 729-1315, thewellingtongastropub.com)*.

Photo: Charles Earl

Elvis Lives . . . in Ottawa's West End

Don't let anyone tell you different: Ottawa is the place where the King of Rock 'n' Roll retired. One of Ottawa's institutions, **Moe's World Famous Newport Restaurant** in Westboro, at the corner of Churchill Avenue and Richmond Road, is owner Moe Attalah's tribute to Elvis Presley. Once you walk through the convenience store, past the snacks and newspapers, the Newport provides high quality, standard American-style fare, including homestyle burgers, pizza, and fish and chips. It's also the official headquarters of the Elvis Sighting Society (check out the Elvis Lives Lane street sign outside, officially designated by city council). Elvis memorabilia covers most of the inside space, and Attalah claims to receive

mail for the King from all over the world (that he refuses to open). The Newport and **Elvis Sighting Society** also hosts a number of community events, including a Christmas dinner. Watch for the Douvris Martial Arts Academy next door, with the sign that claims: "Elvis trains here." Fun facts about the historic Newport are written on their menu; check out the one about American President Bill Clinton's mother, when she came to visit.

334 Richmond Rd., 722-9322

The Wine List

Situated in the back of a row house in the Glebe, **107 Fourth Avenue Wine Bar** *(107 Fourth Ave., 236-0040, 107fourthavenue.com)*, serves 30 or so wines from the glass or bottle for enophiles (on a budget or not). If you're downtown, the classiest place is easily **Vineyards Wine Bar Bistro** (see photo) *(54 York St., 241-4270, vineyards.ca/web)*. Winner of the "Best Wine List in Ottawa" in *Ottawa Magazine*, it boasts over 300 different wines, including a full list online. If you want a bottle of something local and uniquely flavoured, drive to **Strathmore Winery** near the village of Monkland, just 90 minutes east of the city off

Highway 138 *(932-1470)* for some of the best local fruit wine, including blueberry, apple, and apple-cranberry wines. It's still too small a winery to have its product carried in stores, so if you don't get it from them, you just don't get it. Call them for directions.

BEST BREAKFAST

I don't know what it is they do exactly, but there's something they put in the scrambled eggs at the **Baker Street Café** *(385 Richmond Rd., 729-8807)* that makes them uniquely tasty. Don't believe me? Check it out for yourself. On the weekends, you can always try the quiet local ambience of **Pubwells** *(96 Preston St., 236-1175)*. The **Bramasole Diner** *(428 Bank St., 234-0502)* has an all-day breakfast and is known for its "Bram Slams." Otherwise, you can always try old standards **Dunn's Famous Deli** *(220 Elgin St., 230-6444; 203 Queen St., 230-4005)*, the **Elgin Street Diner** *(374 Elgin St., 237-9700, elginstreetdiner.com)*, the only 24-hour spot for good, cheap food (including milkshakes), or the 1950s style of **Zak's Diner** *(14 Byward Market Square, 241-2401, zaksdiner.com)*.

DO YOU WANT GRAVY WITH YOUR PIZZA?

You might not think it sounds appetizing, but once you've been to **House of Georgie & Sorento's Pizzeria** *(211 Gilmour St. at Elgin St., 238-3333, houseofgeorgie. com)* for their "Gravy Pizza," you'll be hooked. Exactly what it sounds like, the House of Georgie sells individual pizza slices covered in a spicy gravy that can excite even the most disinterested palate. There are usually lineups out the door on any given evening — and the later it is, the longer the lineup. If gravy on your pie isn't your thing, they have a good selection of other pizzas as well.

PIZZA WITH PIZZAZZ

Colonnade Pizza *(280 Metcalfe St. at Gilmour St., 237-3179)* has been serving some of the best pizza in Centretown since 1967. The 200-seat restaurant may look nondescript (from the *outside*, anyway), but that's when you know a place is really good. They have other locations, including Kanata *(461 Hazeldean Rd., 831-5599)*, the West End *(1463 Merivale Rd., 727-8686)*, and Ottawa South (for delivery; *1500 Bank St., 737-1107). colonnadepizza.com*

For the Romantics

In the summer, there's nothing like a patio for romantic dining, or even just a drink while talking about nothing at all. Options in the Byward Market include **Bistro 115** *(110 Murray St., 562-7244, bistro115.com)* and the **Black Cat Café** *(93 Murray St., 241-2999, blackcatcafe.ca)*. There are some more high-end places downtown as well, such as **Wilfrid's** at the **Château Laurier** *(reservations recommended; 1 Rideau St., 241-1414, fairmont. ca/laurier)*

or **Le Café** in the **National Arts Centre**, specializing in a variety of Canadian dishes from Atlantic salmon to Alberta beef. The patio has a nice view overlooking the Rideau Canal *(53 Elgin St. by the canal, 594-5127)*. Also worth sampling are the Italian dishes of the **Canal Ritz** *(375 Queen Elizabeth Dr., 238-8998, canalritz.com)* (see photo above).

Viva Italia

Ottawa's Italian neighbourhood was originally an Irish area housing employees of nearby lumberyards before a surge of Italian immigration occurred at the turn of the 20th century. A second wave of Italian immigration that came after World War II turned the area between Booth and Preston Streets, from Carling Avenue north, into Ottawa's **"Corso Italia,"** featuring fine restaurants, shops, street parties, and other activities (watching World Cup soccer in Little Italy is a must). And don't miss out on **La Vendemmia – Ottawa's Celebration of Italian Wine & Food** in September. *prestonstreet.com*

Mangi, Mangi!

Photo: John W. MacDonald

Home to one of the best wine cellars in the city, **Trattoria Caffé Italia** *(254 Preston St., 236-1081, trattoriaitalia.com)* has been run by the Carrozza family for over 20 years; it started life in the 1950s as a billiard and card-laying social club for the Preston Street community. Some other recommended Italian restaurants, all of them located in Corso Italia on Preston Street, include **Ciccio Caffe** *(330 Preston St., 232-1675)*, **Giovanni's** *(362 Preston St., 234-3156)*, **La Dolce Vita** *(180 Preston St., 233-6239)*, **La Roma** *(430 Preston St., 234-8244, laromaottawa.com)*, and **La Vecchia Trattoria** *(228 Preston St., 230-0009)*. For some of the best in cozy romantic dining, including veal and pasta dishes, try **Allegro Ristorante** *(422 Preston St., 235-7454)*.

If high-end Italian isn't your thing, get down to the working class digs of Little Italy's **The Prescott** *(379 Preston St., 232-1136, theprescott.com)* (see photo). One of the oldest taverns in town, it was cleaned up a few years ago – ironically reducing the "gritty tavern" appeal – but they still have some of the best pasta and meatball sandwiches in town.

It's All Greek to Them

Some of the most authentic Greek food in the city can be found at **Papagus Greek Taverna** *(281 Kent St., 233-3626)* or the more upscale establishment of **Theo's Greek Taverna** *(911 Richmond Rd., 728-0909)*. *The Ottawa X-Press* published a promising review in 2005 on Theo's fare and received many responses from beleaguered Grecophiles who claim that Papagus is the most authentic this side of the Mediterranean. But it has been **Greek on Wheels** that has won the magazine's "Best Of Ottawa" readers' poll for eight years in a row now. Offering take out, delivery, and eat-in, the original Greek on Wheels location at 3 Hawthorne Avenue *(235-0056 or 234-7335, greekonwheels.com)* has been a favourite of prime ministers and mayors as well as other local clientele. They now have locations spread

Photo: John W. MacDonald

A PATRIOTIC DELICACY

If you think a beaver tail is nothing more than the back end of a large rodent, then you just don't know anything about Ottawa. Created in 1978 in an homage to fur traders, **Hooker's Beaver Tails** *(beavertailsinc.com)* are a pastry stretched to the shape of a beaver's tail and float-cooked on canola or soya oil, topped with butter, and sprinkled with sugar. You can find them in various places around North America, but in Ottawa you can go straight to the original, along the Rideau Canal during Winterlude or in the heart of the Byward Market, where they have a year-round location at 69 George Street.

If you want something quicker and more traditional, check out **Terry Scanlon's hot dog cart** on the corner of Bank Street at Laurier Avenue, a fixture in front of L'Esplanade Laurier since 1983. As Scanlon described to the *Ottawa Citizen*, "Our technique is, we steam boil the wieners and sausages first. Then we lightly barbeque them after that, and serve with a steamed bun. It's a system we invented."

Now that we've got your attention, **Beckta Dining & Wine** (226 Nepean St., 238-7068, beckta .com) not only fed the Rolling Stones when they performed in Ottawa a few years ago, but they also offer one of the best dining experiences in town for French cuisine. Be prepared to spend about $250 for two people. At least you know both food and wine will be *spectacular.*

Photo of Kinki: Lois Siegel

SUSHI TIME

If sushi is your thing, check out my favourites: **Go For Sushi** (234 Queen St., 288-2288), **Sushi 88** (690-B Somerset St. W., 233-3288, sushi88.ca) and **Wasabi Japanese Restaurant and Sushi Bar** (41 Clarence St., 241-3636). For good but rather pricey sushi in the Byward Market, go to **Kinki** (41 York St., 789-7559, kinki.ca) (see photo above); they even have a two-for-one special during happy hours (3–5 p.m., weekdays).

across Ottawa, including in Orléans (4025 Innes Rd., 824-5900 or 824-9005), Kanata (444 Hazeldean Rd. 836-5757 or 836-7111), South Keys (25 Tapiola Cres., 737-1177), Ottawa East (585 Montreal Rd., 749-1100), and Merivale (1465 Merivale Rd., 225-4999).

And despite all this fanfare, don't overlook **Pilos Restaurant Ottawa** (876 Montreal Rd., 741-4657, pilosrestaurant.com), another Ottawa must for your Greek tooth.

South of Two Borders

To satisfy your Tex-Mex cravings, or simply to get a strawberry margarita, check out **Blue Cactus Bar & Grill** (2 Byward Market Square, 241-7061, bluecactusbarandgrill.com). With upscale décor and an expanded space, Blue Cactus is fine for quiet dining, business events, and private parties; late night weekends also include DJs spinning a mix of soul, funk, and house music. At the same time, there's nothing like the original **Mexicali Rosa's** for doing it so much better, and long before the whole Tex-Mex craze took over the restaurant industry. Check out their original location at 895 Bank (236-9499, mexicalirosas.com) or any of the others they've opened since (including 2401 St Joseph Blvd., 824-6014; 1800 Bank St., 526-1818; 33 Clarence St., 789-1578; 1001 Queen Elizabeth Dr., 234-8156; 115 Roland Michener Dr., 591-0091).

Come for the Food, Stay for the Karaoke

Owned by the Kwan family for three generations, **Shanghai Restaurant** (651 Somerset St. W., 233-4001, shanghaiottawa.com) was the first Chinese restaurant in Chinatown, opening in 1971. It offers great food (including some of the city's best hot and sour soup) and exotic drinks; it also has some of the best karaoke in Ottawa, hosted by **MC Edward Kwan**, a.k.a. "China Doll" (known for wearing a variety of fun, outlandish costumes) and karaoke master Carmen (who has been described as Canada's Andy Warhol). Kwan also moonlights as the head chef. Check out the side of the building for the mural of China Doll by Ottawa artist Melody Hovey.

Other Chinese Food Options

Ben Ben Restaurant: Perfect for lunches (697 Somerset St. W., 238-5022, benbenrestaurant.com).

Cathay: A room full of government workers can't be wrong, especially at their downtown lunch buffet location (228 Albert St., 233-7705; 1423 Woodroffe Ave. [take-out only], 228-2228; 1755 St. Laurent Blvd., 521-9168).

Ruby Inn Ottawa: Not much more than a counter, this infamous take-out joint has been around for decades (1834 Bank St., 731-1873).

So Good: Perfect for lunches, especially for their lunch specials (717 Somerset St. W., 233-0138).

Yang Sheng Restaurant: Great for either the middle of the day or on the way home from the bars, this Chinatown diner has some of the best late-night Cantonese food and casual atmosphere (662 Somerset St. W. [at Bronson Ave.], 235-5794, yangshengrestaurant.com).

Yangtze Restaurant: Some of the finest food in Chinatown, great for taking groups (700 Somerset St. W., 236-0555, yangtze.ca).

Thai Me Up, Thai Me Down

If your feel a hankering for some good Thai food, you can't go wrong with any of these places:

Anna Fine Thai Cuisine: 91 Holland Ave., 759-8472

Chaophraya Thai Cuisine: 1775 Carling Ave. 798-0651

Coriander Thai Cuisine: 282 Kent St., 233-2828

Green Papaya Classic Thai Cuisine: 246 Queen St., 238-8424; 256 Preston St., 231-8424; or their third location across the river, **Papaye Verte:** 69 rue Laurier, Gatineau, 819-777-0404, greenpapaya.ca

Hot Peppers Expressive Thai Cuisine: 495 Somerset St. W., 233-4687; 201 Queen St., 232-4687, hot-peppers.ca

Khao Thai: 103 Murray St., 241-7276, khauthai.ca

Full o' Beans

We might not be like Vancouver, where there's a coffee shop on every single corner, but we still have a number of places to drink a good cup of joe while you clack away on your laptop. Sure, there are plenty

FEE-FI-PHO

Looking for a bowl of that comforting Vietnamese soup known as *pho*? Try any of these late-night places around the city, all of which are very reasonably priced: **Pho Bo** (1053 Somerset St. W., 724-6279), **Pho-Bo-Ga** (12 Lebreton St. N., 234-7521), **Pho Thu Do** (765 Somerset St. W., 235-7116), or **Pho-Bo-Ga 2** (843 Somerset St. W., 234-7089, phoboga2.com). At all three locations, you can get three different serving sizes, depending on your appetite. Fresh-made wraps and a variety of vegetarian dishes are available as well.

MUNCH-A-LUNCH

Being a government town, Ottawa has a whole *slew* of options for lunches. Some of the best take-out sandwiches in town, year after year, can be found at the Italian restaurant/grocer **DiRienzo's Grocery** (1121 Meadowlands Dr., 723-4664; 111 Beech St., 729-4037). Another good spot is **Three Bakers & a Bike** (1281 Wellington St. W., 266-0319), notable for their salads and soups.

of locations for **Tim Hortons, Timothy's, Second Cup,** and **Starbucks**, but keep your eye open for **Bridgehead Coffeehouse**, specializing in fair trade coffee. They're all over the place: including 362 Richmond Road *(729-4401)*, 366 Bank Street *(569-5600)*, 108 Third Avenue *(236-5445)*, 109 Bank Street *(230-8548)*, 131 Beechwood Avenue *(744-3735)*, and 282 Elgin Street *(234-0002)*. (According to my teenage daughter, the one at 109 Bank Street – as well as having the best windows and highest ceilings of any of their locations – is also staffed by the *prettiest boys*.)

Photo: Serge Brousseau

If you're in the neighbourhood, **Café Mio** *(1379 Wellington St. W., 761-5510)* is another coffee spot we would highly recommend. Other caffeine-fix options include **Hava Java** *(279 Elgin St., 233-5282)*, **Planet Coffee** *(24-A York St., 789-6261)*, **Cuppedia Coffees Teas & Delicacies** *(97 Main St., 567-0839)*, and **Roast'n Brew**, with two locations at 251 Laurier Avenue West *(594-5665)* or 51 Queen Street *(569-6462)*; finally, you have to admire **Thanks a Latte** just for its name *(1620 Scott St., 798-5348)*.

And since you asked, the best cappuccino in town has to be at Joe Calabro's **Pasticceria Gelateria Italiana** *(200 Preston St., 233-2104, ottawawedding. com/cakegalleria)*, makers of made-to-design wedding cakes, beautiful pastries, gelato, and lots of different kind of espresso, including Espresso Borgia, which comes compete with orange peel. Established in 1979, their motto is "Perfecting the Fine Art of Confections." Still, if you'd rather stay at home but don't have the equipment, be sure to visit the **Italian Gift Shop** *(785 Gladstone Ave., 233-3719)* for any sort of coffee-making machine.

MUNCH-A-BRUNCH

If you want something a little more upscale than a diner for your brunch, check out **Egg Spectation** *(171 Bank St., 569-6505, eggspectation. ca)*, **Cora's Breakfast & Lunch** *(1530 St Laurent St., 563-2672; 179 Rideau St., 241-7642; 2629 Alta Vista Dr., 523-2672)*, or **Prime 360** *(Minto Pl., 407 Laurier Ave. W., 782-2422, prime-360.com)*. Or you can always head over to Chinatown for dim sum, whether at **Chu Shing** *(691 Somerset St. W., 233-8818)*, or **Yangtze Restaurant** *(700 Somerset St. W., 236-0555, yangtze.ca)*.

Literature & the Arts

Photo: Olga Novoa

When then-mayor Bob Chiarelli threatened to cut all arts funding in the city in 2004, City Councillor Clive Doucet reminded us of Ottawa's historic small-mindedness. In an article in the *Ottawa Citizen*, he invoked Confederation poet Archibald Lampman, who a century ago had predicted the city would become "the Florence of the North." Unfortunately, Ottawa currently has the worst arts funding (per capita) of any major Canadian city. Despite this, Ottawa still has a thriving and robust arts community that is both grassroots and world class.

To Ottawa, With Love

Originally published in 1960 as a short story in the collection of the same name, "For Your Eyes Only" by **Sir Ian Fleming** details the adventures of James Bond, including a drive in his "Hertz Udrive Plymouth saloon along the broad Route 17 from Montreal to Ottawa … trying to remember to keep on the right of the road." Throughout his depictions of Ottawa, Sir Ian favours the word "grey."

Canada's First Literary Capital

Well before Toronto, Montreal, and Vancouver became regarded as the country's main cultural centres, Ottawa was known as one of the literary capitals of the Dominion of Canada. In the few years after Canada became a nation (1867, for those of you who have forgotten your high school social studies class), Ottawa writers **Archibald Lampman** and **Duncan Campbell Scott**, and New Brunswick poet **Charles G. D. Roberts** – a group later called the "Confederation Poets," many of whom lived and worked in the Ottawa area – were giving voice to this new country.

A Morpeth, Ontario native, Lampman published poems frequently in Canadian, American, and British periodicals while working as a low-paid clerk in the post office department in Ottawa from 1883 until he died. He published *Among the Millet, and Other Poems* (1888) at a printing house on Sparks Street; this slim volume of poems on rural life and nature was the first poetry collection published in Ottawa. The book soon established Lampman as the finest English Canadian poet of his time. There is a stained glass window with Lampman's portrait, along with a number of other writers (including Walter Scott and Thomas More), created by Harry Horwood in 1906, currently installed in the Ottawa Public Library main branch at 120 Metcalfe Street. Lampman is buried at Beechwood Cemetery.

Influenced by Victorian and Romantic themes, Duncan Campbell Scott was a short story writer as well as a poet, publishing such books as *The Magic House and Other Poems* (1893) and a collection of short fiction, *In the Village of Viger* (1896). An employee of the Department of Indian Affairs, he incorporated much of his experience and knowledge of the Aboriginal peoples into his work (which, considering how they were treated by his department, is not looked upon terribly favourably). There is a plaque in his honour in front of the ugly 1960s-era building that replaced his home at **108 Lisgar Street**.

For the past few years, the *Ottawa Citizen* has sponsored an annual short story competition named for Scott, the winner of which is announced every year as part of the City of Ottawa literary awards night, which also gives out the Archibald Lampman Award for best book of poetry by an Ottawa resident. Sponsored by *Arc* magazine, the two honours merged in 2007 as the **Lampman-Scott Award for Poetry**.

A Good Place to Sit Down and Weep

When it comes to writers from Ottawa, they don't get any better than **Elizabeth Smart**. Daughter of a prominent lawyer, Smart grew up in Ottawa and socialized with the political and literary figures of the city, including Prime Ministers William Lyon Mackenzie King (the Smarts owned a summer home next to his at Kingsmere) and Lester B. Pearson. Smart's mother was known around the city for her parties (various addresses for Smart over the years include 515 Besserer Street, 15 Linden Terrace, and 361 Daly Avenue). In terms of literary gossip, Smart is known for her relationship with the already-married British poet George Barker; she ended up having four children with him, although he never divorced his wife. Drawing upon a journal from an early age, she documented a fictional account of her relationship with Barker in her wonderfully lyric novel *By Grand Central Station I Sat Down and Wept* (1945), which earned her a cult following as a kind of proto-Beat writer in England and the United States when it was first published, and international acclaim 20 years later, after it had been "re-discovered." All of this was considered scandalous to her mother, who, when the book was first released, actually convinced government officials

GARBAGE COLLECTOR

Ottawa artist **Eric Walker** has always had a fascination with found objects, whether bits of metal, roofing material, or plywood (some picked up off the streets during his regular walks around Centretown). These bits and pieces become part of his art, making "commonly viewed places and things," as he calls his work, which includes panoramic city views, public transit vehicles, government buildings, telecommunication towers, railway cars, and maritime and container ships. Born in Halifax in 1957, he studied at the Nova Scotia College of Art and Design, and counts Patterson Ewen, Robert Frank, June Leaf, Joseph Beuys, Martha Rosler, Allen Sekula, and Dan Graham among his influences. Walker started to exhibit in 1982, moved to Montreal in 1989, and arrived in Ottawa two years later. He has continued to show his work primarily in artist-run galleries locally, nationally, and internationally, including Gallery 101, SAW, and the Ottawa Art Gallery (see pp. 82–83).

OLD FAITHFUL

The oldest active Canadian theatre company, the **Ottawa Little Theatre,** was established in 1913 by the Ottawa Women's University Club, performing in various locations throughout the city. In 1928, the company found a permanent home in the newly remodeled Eastern Methodist Church. During World War II, the main floor was converted into a movie theatre to alleviate financial woes; it continued rehearsals and performances in the basement until 1947, when it reclaimed the main floor of the building. On July 1, 1970, the building burnt down but was replaced two years later by a new theatre.

400 King Edward Ave., 233-8949, o-l-t.com

that it should be banned in Canada, and bought and burned whatever copies she could find that had been imported, just to make sure no decent Canadian could read a copy. After years of silence, Smart started publishing again in the late 1970s with the novel *The Assumption of the Rogues & Rascals* (1977), followed by other books, including two volumes of journals, *Necessary Secrets: The Journals of Elizabeth Smart* (1986). Smart eventually made her home in England where she lived the rest of her life, aside from a brief stint in Edmonton from 1982 to 1983, and a year spent in Toronto. There is a film on her life called *Elizabeth Smart: On the Side of the Angels,* but the best piece on Smart's life is Toronto writer Rosemary Sullivan's magnificent biography, *By Heart: Elizabeth Smart, a Life* (1991), which won the Governor General's Literary Award for nonfiction.

The Mystery of Franklin W. Dixon

Of all the authors from Ottawa, perhaps the most successful is one whose name you've probably never heard: **Leslie McFarlane.** Born in 1902 in Carleton Place, an hour outside of the city, and later a resident on Ottawa's Christie Street during his tenure at the National Film Board, McFarlane ghost-wrote most of the famous *Hardy Boys* children's mystery series under the pseudonym Franklin W. Dixon. Though he wrote approximately 20 of the titles in the series (supposedly his wife wrote the last one under his name), he wasn't paid anything more than a flat fee of $100 per book. He later went on to work for the CBC in Toronto, and

spent a brief time in the United States as a scriptwriter for *Bonanza,* the TV western starring fellow Ottawan Lorne Greene. McFarlane returned to Canada to write a number of books under his own name, including his 1976 autobiography, *The Ghost of the Hardy Boys.* He died in 1977 in Oshawa, Ontario. A more famous McFarlane, perhaps, is his son, Brian McFarlane of CBC's *Hockey Night in Canada,* who not only wrote his own books on hockey, he also invented the iconic cartoon character Peter Puck.

Local Literati

Here are a few contemporary authors that Ottawa can feel proud to call its own.

Charles de Lint

One of the most prolific and admired authors working in the genre of contemporary fantasy lives in Ottawa: the writer (and musician) Charles de Lint, author of more than 60 titles of short fiction as well as novels. His work is even read by British author Neil Gaiman (if you read any fantasy or comic books, that would *really impress you*). Never one to turn his back on his roots, de Lint, along with his wife, used to run a weekly Celtic music jam in the Byward Market, and he's renowned for his annual summer (and very public) sale of books acquired throughout his travels. *charlesdelint.com*

BEST OF THE SMALL PRESS

If you want to know anything about small press publications in Ottawa, the best person to talk to is writer, publisher, editor, bibliographer, and all-round bibliophile **jwcurry**. Well before he moved here from Toronto in 1996, he was called the best concrete and visual poet in Canada. He has over 3 million publications – most notably, perhaps, the largest collection in the world of works by late concrete poet **bpNichol** – carefully filed away in his small Chinatown apartment (a.k.a. **Room 302 Books**, *302– 880 Somerset St. W., 233-0417).* Make an appointment or wander by; he's usually in his window working away at the typewriter (check out the big letter H in his front window). Believe it or not, curry still produces publications by hand stamping, or with his 1926 Gestetner machine (making the place smell like an old high school).

Photo: John W. MacDonald

GONE, BUT NOT FORGOTTEN

Here are a few Ottawa-born authors who left the nest:

Margaret Atwood was born at the Ottawa General Hospital, and she lived with her family on Patterson Avenue in the Glebe until she was about a year old. She currently lives in Toronto and is, of course, one of Canada's preeminent writers of fiction, poetry, and nonfiction.

The youngest child of Carol Shields, **Sara Cassidy** was born in Ottawa while her mother was studying at the University of Ottawa. She is currently a poet, playwright, and fiction writer living in Victoria, BC.

Nicholas Power, who cofounded the Toronto Small Press Book Fair in 1987, is editor and publisher of the literary micro-press Gesture Press. Born and raised in Ottawa, he now lives in Toronto, where he publishes poetry and short fiction.

Priscila Uppal, who moved to Toronto to attend York University, was born and raised in Ottawa. Her narrative-driven verse displays an array of European influences; her fourth poetry collection, *Ontological Necessities* (2006), was shortlisted for the $50,000 Griffin Poetry Prize in 2007.

Elisabeth Harvor

A resident of the Parkdale/Westboro area the past few years, Harvor's earlier writings on family and marriage are based on her own life, when she lived in a house with her husband and children in Sandy Hill. (The house itself was torn down long ago to make way for the Morisset Library at the University of Ottawa.) Her award-winning poetry and fiction titles include *Fortress of Chairs* (1992), which won The Gerald Lampert Memorial Award, and her most recent novel, *All Times Have Been Modern* (2004), which was a finalist for the Ottawa Book Award.

William Hawkins

Ottawa's preeminent poet throughout the 1960s and 70s, "Railroad" Bill Hawkins, ran the famed coffeehouse Le Hibou for years on Sussex Avenue with his wife, Sheila Louise Hawkins. Bill Hawkins was also an influential member of the city's community of folk songwriters, penning lyrics for the band The Children, which featured Sandy Crawley and a young Bruce Cockburn. Perhaps the city's most literary cabbie, Hawkins has worked for Blue Line Taxi since the early 70s. When Broken Jaw Press launched a collection of his work, *Dancing Alone: Selected Poems 1960–1990*, in 2005 (his first poetry collection in over 30 years) at the Ottawa International Writers Festival, it was the largest poetry launch Library and Archives Canada had ever held, with an audience of nearly 300 people to hear his lines of meditative, 60s roughneck sensibilities.

Elizabeth Hay

One of the nicest writers you could ever meet – in Ottawa or anywhere else – much of Hay's recent work places her squarely in Old Ottawa South: rich and meditative fiction that may or may not incorporate aspects of her own life. Her most recent novel, *Late Nights on Air*, won the 2007 Scotiabank Giller Prize, the highest honour for Canadian fiction.

John Newlove

Though a Saskatchewan poet to the core, Newlove lived in Ottawa's Chinatown for 17 years until his death in 2003 – longer than he had lived anywhere else. With his elegiac, sparse poems, Newlove was considered the best lyric poet in Canada from 1964 to 1974 by many of his contemporaries such as George Bowering, Margaret Atwood, and Michael Ondaatje.

All Under One Roof

Originally the Carleton County Courthouse, the **Arts Court Building** (2 Daly Ave., 564-7240, artscourt.ca) has been the site of the community's municipal arts centre since 1988, after being purchased by the Ottawa Arts Court Foundation. Conveniently located between the Rideau Centre and the Ottawa Jail Hostel, the building houses the Ottawa Art Gallery, SAW Gallery, Arts Court Theatre, Opera Lyra, Le Groupe Dance Lab, Salamander Theatre Company (a children's theatre), the Independent Filmmakers Co-operative of Ottawa, Ottawa Fringe Festival, and Ottawa International Animation Festival, as well as the Art Rental and Sales Service. With a waiting list for tenants, there has been talk for a number of years of creating a larger building to house Ottawa's artistic community. The current facility is open seven days a week from 9 a.m. to 10:45 p.m.

So Much Art, So Little Space

Even though they say they don't want another embassy or office building on the site of the former Canada and the World Pavilion on Sussex Drive, the government and the National Capital Commission certainly aren't making it easy for the **Ottawa Art Gallery** (233-8699, ottawaartgallery.ca) to potentially take up new digs in the now-empty space, having long outgrown the Arts Court Building. The lack of space is in part due to the approximately 1,600 paintings, drawings, and sculptures donated to the City of Ottawa by the late O. J. and Isobel Firestone, worth roughly $11 million and including work by, among others, the Group of Seven. The gallery also owns a growing contemporary collection of 250 works by some of the region's best artists, including Mark Marsters, Dennis Tourbin, Evergon, Eric Walker, Lorraine Gilbert, Leslie Reid, Kenneth Lochhead, and Marie-Jeanne Musiol. Unlike galleries in other centres across Canada, much of the money that would otherwise get donated to the OAG goes to national institutions such as the National Gallery of Canada on Sussex Drive. Hard

LOCAL LIT MAGS

Arc: Canada's National Poetry Magazine: publishes a semi-annual collection of predominantly metaphor-driven verse and poetry book reviews (arcpoetry.ca).

Bywords Quarterly Journal: as well as publishing poetry and a literary calendar online every month, the journal publishes work produced in a variety of poetic forms (bywords.ca).

Front & Centre: Ottawa's roughneck fiction magazine, produced by editor and publisher Matthew Firth (ardentdreams.com/blackbilepress/home.html).

Ottawater: since January 2005, the journal has existed only as an online annual, publishing a range of poetic styles, including concrete/visual and nonlinear (ottawater.com).

Puritan Magazine: the University of Ottawa's literary prose journal, distributed free around the city and campus (puritan-magazine.com).

STANZAS: long poems/sequences, distributed free through above/ground press (abovegroundpress.blogspot.com), with nearly 50 issues since 1993.

GAGGLE OF GALLERIES

Here are a few of Ottawa's commercial galleries:

Art Mode Gallery: *531 Sussex Dr., 241-1511, artmode.com*

ArteSol Gallery: *279 Dalhousie St., 789-0874*

Calligrammes Art Gallery: *21 Murray St., 241-4732, calligrammes.com*

Darshan Gallery: *113 Murray St., 241-7020*

Galerie St-Laurent + Hill: *333 Cumberland St., 789-7145, galeriestlaurentplushill.com*

gallery four seven nine: *479 Sussex Dr., 244-0479, galleryfoursevennine.com*

Gallery of the Kanadas: *21 Clarence St., 789-9591, kanadas.ca*

Wallack Galleries, *203 Bank St., 235-4339, wallackgalleries.com*

INDY ART

Some of the more interesting ground-level artwork can often be found at such offbeat places as **ArtGuise** *(509 Bank St., 238-3803, artguise. ca)*, **Cube Gallery** *(7 Hamilton Ave. N., 728-1750, cubegallery. ca)*, **Dale Smith Gallery** *(137 Beechwood Ave., 321-0101, dalesmithgallery.com)*, **Pukka Gallery** *(430 Parkdale Ave., 761-1515, pukkagallery.ca)*, **Shanghai Restaurant** *(651 Somerset St. W., 233-4001, shanghaiottawa.com)*, or the **Manx Pub** *(370 Elgin St., downstairs, 231-2070)*.

Photo: John W. MacDonald

to believe in a town this size, with its history going back as long as it does, that the OAG will be only 20 years old in 2008, originally started by a group of local artists who felt that the city should have its own gallery.

SAW

Founded in 1974 as Sussex Annex Works at a location on Sussex Avenue, **SAW Gallery** *(Tue.–Sat., 11 a.m.–6 p.m.; galeriesawgallery.com)* moved to its present home inside the Arts Court Building in 1988. It is an artist-run centre which currently houses a gallery for contemporary painting and installation works, SAW Video, and a performance space.

SAW Sister

After existing above Wallack's Art Supplies at Bank and Lisgar for years before moving to 236 Nepean Street, **Gallery 101**, Ottawa's sister artist-run centre to SAW, was forced to move again to 301½ Bank Street *(Tues.–Sat., 10 a.m.–5 p.m.; 230-2799, gallery101.org)*.

What Happens in Canada, Doesn't Necessarily Stay in Canada

It would be impossible to talk about art in the capital without mentioning the **National Gallery of Canada** *(380 Sussex Dr., 990-1985, gallery.ca)*. Home to the city's premiere collection of contemporary art for over a century, the National Gallery was founded in 1880 by then-Governor General John Douglas Sutherland Campbell, ninth Duke of Argyll, and has weathered a number of storms over the years, including the 1989

Photo: Charles Earl

purchase of American artist Barnett Newman's *Voice of Fire* (controversial for its $1.8 million price tag, and its simplicity – a red stripe on a blue background) and the 1991 showing of Jana Sterbak's infamous *Vanitas: Flesh Dress for an Albino Anorectic* (or "Meat Dress" – 50 pounds of salted flank steak, stitched together and draped on a mannequin). Some of the highlights of the permanent collection include a church situated inside the building, works by Canadian artists Roy Kiyooka, Greg Curnoe, and David Milne, and an entire room that had been painted (and recreated in the gallery) by members of the Group of Seven. There are also a number of pieces by Warhol, Matisse, Chagall, Picasso, and Rubens.

Still, if you want to see quality Canadian art but aren't a fan of the crowds, you could always head over instead to the **Carleton University Art Gallery** *(St. Patrick's Building, 1125 Colonel By Dr., 520-2120, carleton.ca/gallery)*, which also has an impressive series of shows, as well as a large collection of contemporary and recent Canadian art, including a rich variety of Inuit and First Nations works.

Master of the Portrait

The world-famous Ottawa-based photographer **Yousuf Karsh** is perhaps best known for his 1941 photograph of a glowering Winston Churchill; Karsh elicited this unforgettable expression from Sir Winston by snatching the great man's cigar from his mouth without warning. Since named a Companion of the Order of Canada, Karsh further gained international prominence with countless photos of other public figures, such as Albert Einstein, Humphrey Bogart, King George VI, H. G. Wells, George Bernard Shaw, Martin Luther King, Andy

CIVIC SONNETS

Believe it or not, the City of Ottawa was the first Canadian city to appoint an official municipal **poet laureate**. Ottawa poet Dr Catherine Ahearn conceived the idea of the honorary position in 1981 to "help promote the City of Ottawa as well as enrich the lives of its citizens." She sold the idea to then-Mayor Marian Dewar, who then named Ahearn herself the first Ottawa poet laureate in 1982. Ahearn, for her three-year, dollar-a-year position, was to write six poems annually, and attend various civic and community group functions across the city. Through this, she wrote small pieces on the Ottawa River, and on Prince Charles and Lady Diana Spencer, in her self-published *Poet Laureate Poems, 1982–1984*.

Photo: Janet Brooks

The position was later held by poet, fiction writer, and University of Ottawa professor Cyril Dabydeen, and former *Anthos* magazine and Anthos Books editor/publisher Patrick White, who moved to Perth, Ontario in 1988, not five months after being named Poet Laureate. After White's tenure was completed in 1990, the position was quietly eliminated. Since then, poet laureates have been appointed in major cities across Canada; the position of national poet laureate was created in 2002, awarded to Vancouver writer George Bowering (see photo above), who received $12,000 a year, as well as an office and a secretary on Parliament Hill.

Yousuf Karsh photograph by Lois Siegel

Warhol, and Ernest Hemingway (his portraits of John F. Kennedy and Churchill later appeared on the covers of *Life*). Born in Mardin, Armenia, in 1908, he was brought to Canada in 1924 by his uncle, and schooled briefly in Sherbrooke, Quebec. Karsh apprenticed with John Garo of Boston, one of the top portrait photographers in America, before opening his own studio on Sparks Street in 1932. With the help of Prime Minister William Lyon MacKenzie King, the relatively unknown photographer was able to snag visiting dignitaries for their portraits. For 60 years, people famous in politics, theology, royalty, the arts, the sciences, and the military posed for a "Karsh of Ottawa" portrait. His work is in the permanent collections of the Museum of Modern Art and Metropolitan Museum of Art in New York, the Art Institute of Chicago, the National Portrait Gallery in London, and the National Gallery of Canada (see p. 83). The bulk of his work, amounting to some 250,000 negatives, 12,000 colour transparencies, and 50,000 original prints, was sold in 1987 to the National Archives of Canada. He died in 2002.

Shock Art

Arguably one of the most engaging, talented, and difficult artists to come out of Ottawa in the 1990s is **Rob Nelms**. Said to be related to (and cut off from) the Ottawa-based Nelms Opticians family, he was a notorious figure throughout the city for a number of years. Bizarre stories about his artistic feats floated around: he once nailed his penis to a wall, and has hung chunks of metal, large pieces of wood, and even plastic 35mm film canisters from his stretched earlobes. He produced huge amounts of artwork under various pseudonyms (including Emily Whist) and coordinated shows in locations around the city, such as the performances by experimental noise band Kitten Ling Foundation. His art could be found everywhere at that time, including stickers in the washrooms at the University of Ottawa, solo shows at the Mercury Lounge and Artguise, and in various handmade items left on friends' doorsteps. In the early 1990s, he (supposedly) moved to Montreal to enroll in fine arts courses at Concordia University. Over the past few years, various people have asked the question: Whatever happened to Rob Nelms? A possible answer: a recent episode of Kink, the Showcase TV reality series about sex, featured a transgendered woman named "Chicken" who looks suspiciously like Nelms, wandering the street looking for bits of material to produce more artwork.

Cold War Modernist

One of Ottawa's premier conceptual artists, **Adrian Göllner** was born in Germany as an army brat. A former President of the Board of **Artengine**, an online centre for visual and media artists *(artengine.ca)*, he has shown work around Ottawa for years, as well as solo exhibitions from Calgary to Dublin. Combining his interest in abstraction, advertising, and the Cold War, he self-published a series of trading cards, the *Cold War Cards*, which were included in an exhibition at the Diefenbunker (see p. 38) in 2000. In 2003, his show "Modern U." *(modernu.net)* opened at the Carleton University Art Gallery (see p. 84), exploring the campus's modern architecture built during its early development (1959–72). Created in a distinctly modern style, Carleton was purposely absent of vine-covered towers

OTTAWA IN PRINT
The **Ottawa Public Library**, on their website, have compiled an ever-growing list of fiction and nonfiction titles that mention Ottawa, including Norman Levine's **Canada Made Me** (1958), André Alexis' **Childhood** (1998), Alan Cumyn's **Burridge Unbound** (2000), Gerald Lynch's **Exotic Dancers** (2001), Priscila Uppal's **The Divine Economy of Salvation** (2002), Elizabeth Hay's **Garbo Laughs** (2003), and Marwan Hassan's **As the Crow Dies** (2005).
biblioottawa.library.ca

like those at McGill University in Montreal or Queen's in Kingston. Former President Claude Bissell described the new university's vision as *"Brave New World* without the Gothic."* That would explain that cold feeling I always get when I go to the university (plus the fact I constantly get lost in the tunnels). *adriangollner.ca*

Other Local Artists

You can't say anything about the Ottawa community of visual artists without mentioning the late **Mark Marsters**. An instructor at the **Ottawa School of Art** *(35 George St., 241-7471, artottawa.ca)* for a number of years, he worked on a series of narrative paintings that read almost as stories themselves. You can still see some of his outdoor pieces (including the Ottawa map across a large hand) along sections of the Transitway between Tunney's Pasture and Westboro, heading west from the O-Train station *(artottawa.ca/gallery.markmarsters.html)*.

Born in Montreal, writer and curator **Deborah Margo** has been teaching painting and sculpting at the University of Ottawa since 1999, and, for the past 20 years, has exhibited work all across North America, including shows at the Owens Gallery at Mount Allison University (2005), the **Ottawa Art Gallery** (2006), Kingston's Modern Fuel Gallery (2006) and Ottawa's **Cube Gallery** (2006) *(deborahmargo.ca)*.

Working with mixed media, **Amy Thompson** studied fine art at York University, graduated from the Ontario College of Art and Design, and has shown her work in Ottawa, Toronto, New York, Chicago, San Francisco, and Paris. No one else can work old wallpaper, pornographic playing cards, and little bird collages like *she* can *(amyalice.com)*.

Photographer, painter, and printmaker **Jennifer Dickson** was already an internationally acclaimed artist before coming to Canada from South Africa in 1969. Working with still photography, she is perhaps

MIGHTIER THAN THE SWORD

American expatriate **John Bart Gerald** was born in New York City in 1940; he worked with Dr Albert Schweitzer in 1960, and marched with Dr Martin Luther King Jr in 1965 from Selma to Montgomery, Alabama. He and his wife, artist Julie Maas, launched a small press, Gerald and Maas, which published *The Crime of Genocide & Bill of Human Rights* (one of the first documents to spell out a definition of "genocide") with supporting UN texts when it went out of print at the United Nations in 1989. After years of living in Maine, he moved his family to Ottawa in 1995, where he is still very involved in writing, publishing, and activism. He and his wife run an atelier/showroom out of their house at 206 St. Patrick Street *(241-1312, nightslantern .ca)*, where one can peruse their various publications, as well as Maas' artworks, all available for sale.

the most prominent visual artist currently working in the city, with dozens of shows worldwide, including solo shows at the National Gallery of Canada, the Centre Culturel Canadien (Paris), and the Canadian Museum of Contemporary Photography (see p. 37). She is the recipient of dozens of international awards and honours, including the Order of Canada, and was, in 1976, the only Canadian in the 200-year history of the Royal Academy of Art to be elected a Royal Academician.

Troubled Soul

"SPRING FLIGHT"   BENJAMIN CHEE CHEE

Born on Bear Island, Temagami Reserve in northeastern Ontario, Ojibwa artist **Benjamin Chee Chee** was an acclaimed self-taught visual artist who lived for years in Ottawa, influenced both by Aboriginal styles (he was an important member of the second generation of Woodland Indian painters from the 1960s) and modern abstraction. A troubled soul, he managed to produce original artwork while plagued by inner demons. Legend has it that Chee Chee would produce works of art on napkins to trade for a drink or two at taverns such as the old Gilmour (what is now a Rogers Video, at Gilmour and Bank Streets). At the age of 32, at the height of his success as an artist and a printmaker, Chee Chee tragically committed suicide in 1977. A number of his prints are still available, and his artwork is held in collections and galleries, including the Canadian Museum of Civilization (see p. 36). One of Ottawa's poet laureates, Patrick White, published his collection *The Benjamin Chee Chee Elegies* in 1992. Another book, *Chee Chee: A Study of Aboriginal Suicide*, by Al Evans, appeared in 2004.

FRESH FROM THE OVEN

Started as a community of artist spaces in 1993 in a 1920s-vintage bread factory on Gladstone Avenue, the **Enriched Bread Artists' Studio** has been one of the premier spots to see the development of local talent in Ottawa. Way back when, the Standard Bread Company president G. Cecil Morrison had searched for some time before selecting a site that would bring his company closer to the city's limits (right over the current O-Train bridge from Preston St.). As the Depression affected wheat prices, Morrison was fired as president in 1932. The building, which had been empty for some time, is currently home to studios of up-and-coming and established artists in the city. Their annual open house in October easily boasts a thousand visitors. They have recently started hosting events throughout the rest of the year as well, including smaller single-artist shows.
951 Gladstone Ave., 729-7632, artengine.ca/eba

ORCHESTRAL MANOEUVRES

The **National Arts Centre Orchestra** is a busy orchestra. When not at home at the National Arts Centre, it is travelling across the country playing in top theatres and elementary schools as well as performing internationally. Nearing its 40th anniversary, the 50-member orchestra, led by conductor Pinchas Zukerman, currently gives over 100 performances a year and participates in developing successful education programs for young musicians and composers. Supporting new music and making classical tunes accessible to the masses, NACO also collaborates with Canadian pop favourites, such as Steven Page of the Barenaked Ladies and fiddler Natalie MacMaster. *nac-can.ca*

DO ART YOURSELF

If art supplies or framing is what you need, check out any of the Wallack's (see p. 34) locations and Artguise (see p. 83), as well as **Loomis Art Store** *(499 Bank St., 238-3303)* or **Patrick Gordon Framing** *(160 Elm St., 232-7146)*. If you make art and need some money, you can always try approaching the federal arts funding agency, the **Canada Council for the Arts** *(350 Albert St., 566-4414, canadacouncil.ca)*.

Arts for the Nation

NATIONAL ARTS CENTRE
CENTRE NATIONAL DES ARTS

The **National Arts Centre**, Canada's premiere institution for the performing arts, currently houses a concert hall and two theatres for music and the performing arts, and is home to world-class orchestra, theatre, and dance programs, with more than 800 performances each year. Built on the spot where the Russell Theatre opened in 1897 (destroyed by fire) and later, site of the Russell Opera House (torn down in 1928 by the city to make way for what is now Confederation Square), the current building opened in 1969 as the National Arts Centre. With underground parking and a canal-side café, you could spend a whole evening there if you're so inclined. The patio has landscaped terraces with panoramic views of Ottawa and the Rideau Canal. Guided tours are free of charge. *53 Elgin St. at Confederation Square, 996 5051, nac-can.ca*

Expanding Greatness

Now over 30 years old, the **Great Canadian Theatre Company** *(gctc.ca)* produces some of the best in locally and nationally written and produced theatre in Ottawa, with regular commissions from emerging and established stage writers (including a playwright-in-residence) such as Greg Nelson, Colin Heath, Michael Healey, Pierre Brault, and Hannah Moscovitch. For years they were on Gladstone Avenue, west of Preston and a block east of the Enriched Bread Artists' Studio (see p. 88), but check out their newly built digs, the Irving Greenberg Theatre Centre, at 1233 Wellington Street at Holland Avenue with an expanded theatre and better seating.

Maybe the Tin Man Has Deep Pockets

New Ottawa queer theatre company **Toto Too Theatre** *(tototoo.ca)* describes itself as being "committed to the exploration of the gay, lesbian, bisexual, and transgender culture." Before Toto Too appeared, a number of attempts in queer dramatic arts in Ottawa had come and gone, most recently the gay theatre company **Act Out** that, after four years, closed down in 2005 with a debt of $15,000, reminiscent of the local queer film and video festival, **Making Scenes**, which went under in October 2004, also due to finances.

Th-th-th-that's All Folk!

The original Toronto Folklore Centre was a retail space and gathering place for musicians launched by US draft dodger Eric Nagler, who worked with the famed Sharon, Lois & Bram. The **Ottawa Folklore Centre** was opened later and is currently still run by Arthur McGregor, one of the Toronto store's managers. The current Ottawa incarnation sells musical instruments (including mandolins, banjos, acoustic and electric guitars, percussion instruments, and violins – new and used), as well as books and other useful items (whether bagpipe accessories, drums from around the world, or a wide variety of CDs by local and international musicians). It also offers an array of music classes available through the **Ottawa Folklore Centre School of Music.** *1111 Bank St., 730-2887, ottawafolklore.com*

A Dying Art Form

Photo: Charles Earl

In the early 1990s, Ottawa graffiti artist **GO FISH** turned Byward Market and Centretown into exhibition space for his own work, whether mural or large illustration, bringing his art to the world instead of waiting for the world to come to him. Given some of the recent city bylaws pertaining to graffiti, one of the rare locations left in the city where it is still "tolerated" is along the side of the **Ottawa Technical High School** building facing the park on Albert Street, just east of Bronson Avenue (you can catch a glimpse from any public bus). Otherwise, the city will likely paint over the handiwork and charge its artists for the cost. What happened to public art? You can also check out the annual **House of Paint** event that occurs (another "tolerated" public art space) under the Dunbar Bridge near Carleton University (hop.artform.ca).

FOLK FAME

Just outside the Ottawa Folklore Centre is the outdoor sidewalk that makes up the **Canadian Folk Music Walk of Fame** (folkwalk. ca), which was first launched in 2003 with the unveiling of six bronze maple leaf-shaped plaques bearing the names of Canadian folk music legends Stan Rogers, Bruce Cockburn (originally from the suburb of Vanier), Gordon Lightfoot, Joni Mitchell, Jean Carignan, and Helen Creighton. Leonard Cohen and Estelle Klein have since been added to the pantheon. Be sure to check out the lovely mural on the corner of Bank Street and Sunnyside Avenue when you're down there, or even the old mural of fiddles by artist James Stephens on Bronson Avenue (right by Rasputin's Folk Café at 696 Bronson Ave.).

ART IN THE PARK

Founded in 1993 and organized by Ottawa artist Bhat Boy, Art in the Park happens on a Saturday in June every year as a two-day arts festival in the Glebe. Occupying the park along Strathcona Avenue, the event includes visual artists and artisans of all sorts selling and displaying their works, as well as musical acts, dancing, buskers, and theatrics. For anyone interested, artist registration is juried, and often fills up months in advance; check the website for specific information that changes from year to year. *artinfoboy.org*

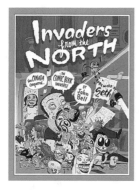

COMIC RELIEF

Ottawa has always been a hotbed of strange underground comic book artists, from the "drunk boy" exploits of **Greg Kerr** to the slacker narratives of **Gavin McInnes** (who went on to invent what became the irreverent, hip hop-driven *Vice Magazine*), or underground legend (and all around nice guy) **David Cooper** (*davegraphics.com*), who had a book of his illustrations introduced by comedian David Cross and another introduced by film director David Cronenberg. Cooper's works include *Underbelly, Weasel, Ripple, Crumple, Dan and Larry*, and *Suckle*. Ottawa is also home to a more mainstream comic artist: **Tom Fowler**, who has published work in *Mad* magazine's *Munroe, Revolution on the Planet of the Apes, Grendel, Green Arrow, Star Wars: Jango Fett* and *Batman: Legends of the Dark Knight*. Also, Ottawa archivist and writer **John Bell** published a book in 2007 about the Canadian presence in the world of comic books, *Invaders from the North: How Canada Conquered the Comic Book Universe*.

Festival Fun

Here are a few arts festivals in Ottawa worth checking out.

Westfest Ottawa

The only free festival in the city featuring big-name artists from the music industry, Westfest is Westboro Village's festival of music and art. Founded in 2003 as a one-day affair, the festival had, by 2006, become a three-day celebration of music, visual art, literature, dance, spoken word, and performance art featuring a spectacular mix of local and national talent, including Susannah M. Smith, Kathleen Edwards, Danny Michel, the Fiftymen, Suki Lee, Matthew Firth, the Cowboy Junkies, and Emm Gryner. With kiosks representing much of the area's business community, the festival takes up the entire street along Richmond Road between Tweedsmuir and Golden Avenues during the second weekend of June. *westfest.ca*

Neil McLeod at Westfest, photographed by John W. MacDonald

Old Ottawa South Art Festival

Founded in 2005, this festival hosts a series of exhibits, artistic activities for children, and a performing stage by artists living, working, or attending school in the Old Ottawa South or Old Ottawa East areas. Arts on display include painting, drawing, mixed media, photography, sculpture, carving, and pottery. Events take place on a Saturday in September every year in Windsor Park, just off Riverdale Avenue, north of Billings Bridge. *oosartfestival.ca*

Adult's Hats $8.-

From bookstores to foodstuffs, Ottawa has everything you need (within reason), if you know where to look for it. Need an Armenian flag, leather bustier, or gourmet fruit jelly? No problem; we can provide all that and more.

Going to Market

Photo: Vlastimil Juricek

Established by Rideau Canal builder Lieutenant-Colonel John By in 1826, the **Byward Market** is one of Canada's oldest and largest public markets. By designated George and York Streets to be wider in order to accommodate the increased traffic of the market where, within an area roughly four blocks wide, you can purchase fresh fruits and vegetables as well as items like maple sugar. Non-edibles also abound, including handmade T-shirts and jewelry. Or you can sample the numerous cafés, restaurants, museums, galleries, pubs, specialty food shops, and the buskers and nightlife the market has to offer, or go straight to the centre of it, at the Byward Market Square building at 55 Byward Market. From May to Labour Day every year, Byward Market Ambassadors (244-4410) are available if you need a more personal touch to your visit. byward-market.com

Gigantic Garage Sale

For 20 years, thousands have flocked to the Glebe for the annual **Great Glebe Garage Sale**, usually held every year on the last Saturday of May. Starting at 9 a.m. and running (roughly) to 3 p.m., the streets can sometimes get so congested with people that it's impossible to get even a bicycle through. Check out the hundreds of tables in front yards and porches throughout this neighbourhood that features a mixture of upscale residents and a large student population (from nearby Carleton University). The sale happens rain or shine, so be sure to bring an umbrella and plenty of cash (the ATM machines in the area empty pretty early). It's worth noting that all participants are asked to donate 10 percent of proceeds to the **Ottawa Food Bank**. If nothing else, it's a great way to spend the day walking around the neighbourhood and meeting people. *theglebeonline.com/garagesale*

Ryan Baylin, Martha Garrett, Ashlee Conery, and Wesley Hughes photographed by Lois Siegel

It's a Mall World

The $250-million **Rideau Centre** mall opened in the spring of 1983 and remains the largest mall in the downtown core, comparable only to **St Laurent Centre** and **Place D'Orléans** in the east end and the **Bayshore** in the west end. With three levels and over 180 stores, this is the central hub of all downtown activity, linking buses from east, west, and south, connecting the Byward Market to Centretown and Sandy Hill. For a number of years, starting the year the mall opened, the two-block stretch along Rideau Street, from Sussex Drive to Dalhousie Street, restricted traffic to buses and taxis as a way to revitalize the local businesses and neighbourhood, but it caused such traffic chaos in the

BYWARD FAMILY MATTERS

One of the events hosted by the Byward Market is the **Mother-Daughter Look-Alike Contest** in May of every year. Come and see what was once something to be feared that was turned into a popular community event. And for dads – or bored seven-year-olds – the **Byward Market Auto Classic** happens on the first Sunday in June, and features an excellent collection of over 150 privately owned classic and collector automobiles. For car owners, the registration is $20 (donated to the Rideau Street Youth Initiative). *byward-market.com/events*

GOTH GEAR

One of the highlights of the Rideau Centre is **Trivium** *(232-2424, trivium.ca)*, situated on the first level. With modern goth, medieval, and sexy, S&M-esque clothing for men and women, the store features unique sneakers and platform boots, corsets, and other studded accessories. The irreverent side is not just for teens anymore.

Photo: Hanif Bayat

GONE WITH THE MUSIC

For any of your new and used musical instrument needs, two of the finest options in the city are **Steve's Music Store** (308 Rideau St., 789-1131, stevesmusic.com) and **Song Bird Music** (388 Gladstone Ave., 594-5323, songbirdmusic.com). With many of the staff in both stores being musicians themselves, you're sure to get some knowledgeable help (and don't worry, most aren't as cranky as they might pretend). See if you can spot musician/author (formerly of the Whirleygigs and the Unbeatables) Alex Mortimer, Slo' Tom, and former Furnaceface frontman Tom Stewart, or the Hilotrons' Paul Hogan or Phil Shaw Bova. Song Bird also has an in-house service department for instrument repairs.

area that it had the opposite affect, driving even more shoppers to suburban malls. Not the only problem by a long shot, the enclosed sidewalks became dank, smelly tunnels that were a haven for mostly harmless street people, and a graveyard for business. After a decade, the tunnels were demolished.
rideaucentre.net

Rideau Street Shops & Stops

Not only the central point for the bus routes, Rideau Street itself is home to a whole range of businesses, including Ottawa's downtown Scottish bar, the **Highlander Pub** (115 Rideau St., 562-5678); **Rock Junction**, for all your rock T-shirt needs (151 Rideau St., 562-3811); **Original Universal Tattoo Studio** (156 Rideau St., 236-3866); **Vertigo Records** (193 Rideau St., 241-1011), the arthouse **ByTowne Cinema** (325 Rideau St., 789-FILM, ottawa.film-can.com); remaindered and used titles at **All Books** (327 Rideau St., 789-9544); and **Nate's Deli**, a favourite of the late Prime Minister Pierre Trudeau (316 Rideau St., 789-9191). *downtownrideau.com*

Back in the Groove

If it's old vinyl you want, the place you have to check out is **Birdman Sound** (593B Bank St., 233-0999, birdmansound.com). Run by John Westhaver, former frontman for the Ottawa punk legends Resin Scraper, this store is Ottawa's longest-running punk record store, with a huge selection of new and used garage, street, and skate punk, and rockabilly vinyl (and a small section of CDs as well), plus a decent selection of jazz, blues, and country. Westhaver also hosts a radio show with local musician Chris Page on Friday mornings on CKCU (93.1 FM, Carleton University) from 9:30 a.m. to 1 p.m. For other used vinyl and CDs (with some carrying new), you should check out **Vertigo Records** *(193 Rideau St., 241-1011, vertigorecords.ca)*, **CD Exchange** *(142 Rideau St., 241-9864, cdexchange.ca)*, or the large selection in the family-owned (two brothers) **Turning Point** *(411 Cooper St., 230-4586, turningpointmusic.ca)*, with an entire second floor of used vinyl to go through.

For new releases by local bands, one of the best places to go is **End Hits** *(407 Dalhousie St., 241-4487, endhits.ca)*, run by Dave Ward and legendary concert promoter Shawn Scallen (who also runs *punkottawa. com*); consignment welcome. Another good place for new titles (local and otherwise) is **Compact Music**, with two locations *(190 Bank St., 233-7626; 785 Bank St., 233-8922; compactmusic.ca)*, or if all else fails, get to the large **HMV** at the corner of Bank Street in the Sparks Street Mall *(233-5483, hmv.ca)*, but don't expect to find as many titles by local musicians there.

Dalhousie Street Smarts

In the Byward Market area is the Dalhousie Street boutique strip, known for its independent and fashionable trend setters, this district is growing fast. Here are some must-do's on your list, in no particular order:

Victoire-ious

Calling itself a "fashion haven for rebel girls with good manners," **Victoire Clothing** *(238 Dalhousie St., 321-1590)* mixes punk aesthetics with fine china, offering not only sweetheart dresses for meeting the parents but also sassy minis for the hot date afterward. Featuring predominantly new clothing, including from Toronto designers, and accessories (such as tea cups and slouchy bags) for any girl who refuses to be pigeonholed. They also have hosted a vintage shoe shopping party, attracting shoe collectors from Montreal.

TILLEY HATS ... AND SO MUCH MORE

A mainstay of Ottawa shopping is **Irving Rivers**, which has "cornered the market" (meaning the Byward Market) for over half a century. Their small space is packed full of travel accessories, backpacks, camping gear, flags (Canadian and international), work clothing, army surplus, and hats of all kinds that it is near-impossible to even turn around (with some stock literally hanging from the ceiling). Come see where Ottawa cartoonist Greg Kerr (while drunk) once bought a pair of Czechoslovakian winter pants so large they could have fit three more of him.

24 Byward Market (at York), 241-1415, irvingrivers.com

A-A-Adorable

Check out Victoire's close neighbours **Attic Clothing** (203 Dalhousie St., 860-0087) and **Amuse** (246 Dalhousie St., 562-2229), which have some of the best original and vintage clothing and collectibles. And for Asian accessories, visit **Abacus Trade** (204 Dalhousie St., 236-4242) which procures fairly traded products from local artisans of Afghanistan, India, Indonesia, Pakistan, and Thailand, from jewelry to fine silks.

Work It

Skip and hop back toward Amuse and Victoire, and you'll find **Workshop Studio & Boutique** (242½ Dalhousie St., 789-5534) which sells handcrafted accessories, handbags, clothes, and unique gifts; and as the name suggests, it also offers workshops to get your thimble nimble (sorry for the pun, but how could you not?).

Mais Inaas Lastname Kiryakos

Such is the acronym for **Milk** (234 Dalhousie St., 789-6455), owned by sisters Mais and Inaas. This independent boutique located beside Victoire is decidedly minimalist yet colourful with its men's and women's apparel and delectable accessories.

Duds for Dudes

For sharp-dressed men, there are the obvious choices, including **Harry Rosen** in Rideau Centre (230-7232, harryrosen.com), **Holt Renfrew** (240 Sparks St., 238-2200), and **Moore's Clothing for Men** (162 Bank St., 235-2121; 2210 Bank St., 738-7090; 2525 Carling Ave., 726-0450; 2280 City Park Dr., 745-0046). But if you want to get noticed, step into **Rugged Culture** (189 Rideau St., 244-3330, ruggedcultureinc.com) for one-stop shopping for everything hip-hop and urban chic (including CDs, DVDs, and accessories). If you're looking for more casual street apparel, one of Ottawa's best sources is **Norml Clothing** (41½ William St., 562-2043, normlclothing.ca). Calling itself a "luxury street boutique," the store also promotes interesting musical events. There's also **Neon Clothing** (45 William St.,

A BYWARD ALTERNATIVE

A bit west of the downtown core, along Parkdale Avenue just north of Wellington Street West, the **Parkdale Market** offers a smaller and more local version of the larger Byward: seasonal fruits and vegetables from various local farms, including pumpkins for Halloween, and even evergreens for Christmas. After your stroll through the Market, treat yourself to a draft beer, a meal, and a game of darts in Sam and Simon's Carleton Tavern (see p. 126) at the corner of Parkdale and Armstrong.

562-2020) for a wide array of youth-oriented jeans, and **Schad** *(527 Sussex Dr., 562-1320)* for coveted New York styles and funky Canadian and European designs.

Dreaming of a Well-Supplied Christmas?

If you want to get your Christmas shopping done well in advance head to the **Christmas Shoppe on William Street** *(71 William St., 789-7171)* as well as the **Christmas Train Store** *(7 Kakulu Rd., Kanata, 592-9402)*, both of which are open year round. During the *actual* holiday season, there are lots of places around the city where you can get holiday supplies, including the perfect Christmas tree. If you'd rather cut your own, check out **Ian's Evergreen Plantation**, just south of the village of Richmond, between Prospect and Franktown. Open from 9 a.m. until dark; bring your own handsaw and cut a fresh tree for $22 (prices vary for different kinds of trees and heights). They have free hayrides and other activities – plus, hot chocolate while you wait for your tree to be cleaned and baled. Check the website for driving instructions from Ottawa (it's about a 35-minute ride). They're open seven days a week, from December 1 through 24. *iansevergreen.on.ca*

Smoke 'em if You Got 'em

For a fine Cuban, or simply to practice your "bad landlord/ crazy old bachelor neighbour" impressions ("You better not have any pets up there!" or "You kids, get off my lawn!"), be sure to check the wide range of cigar emporiums in Ottawa, including **Ottawa Cigar Emporium** *(110B Clarence St., 321-7142, ottawacigar. com)*, **O'Connor Smoke Shop** *(95 O'Connor St., 594-3408)*, **Tony's Cigar Store** at *(233 Elgin St., 235-3841)*, **Comerford's Cigar Store** *(124 Bank St., 232-7448)*, and **Globe Mags & Cigars** *(57 William St., 241-7274)*. Why does Ottawa have so many? Not that you should be smoking anyway.

ANTIQUING

The **Ottawa Antique Market** is open year-round at 1179 Bank Street *(730-6000)*, with china, antiques, jewelry, furniture, and just about anything else you can think of. Other spots worth checking out are **Bentley Antiques & Collectibles Flea Market** at 7 Cleopatra Drive *(225-5613)*, or the **Capital Flea Market** at 2230 Gladwin Crescent behind St. Laurent Boulevard *(513-5000)*, open weekends from 9 a.m. to 5 p.m.

Between the Covers

(see p. 67)

OFF THE BEATEN PATH

It may not be the *main* street, but Main Street, just over the Pretoria Bridge from the south end of Elgin Street, is home to some interesting businesses, well worth the visit. Check out the health food store **The Wheat Berry (Le Grain de blé)**, *(206 Main St., 235-7580)*, the **Green Door Restaurant** (see p. 67) *(198 Main St., 234-9597)*, and **Singing Pebble Books** *(202A Main St., 230-9165, singingpebblebooks.ca)*, which all complement each other quite nicely, in a good-for-you kind of way.

THE MODERN WOMEN'S WEAR

If fair trade and environmentally friendly clothing is what you're after, be sure to check out the Ottawa location of **Karma Wear** at 110 Parent Avenue *(789-0441, karmawearinc.com)*, specializing in "hemp, bamboo, soy, and organic cotton clothing for men and women." If you have money to spare (or even if you don't), be sure to check out the unique contemporary designs of clothes, shoes, and accessories at **Kaliyana Artwear** at 515 Sussex Drive *(562-3676, kaliyana.com)*.

After Stonewall

Ottawa's premier location for gay and lesbian books *(370 Bank St., 567-2221, afterstonewallbooks.com)*. The store's name is a reference to the Stonewall riots in New York City in 1969, a watershed moment for the worldwide gay rights movement. Owner Dave Rimmer is a pillar of the local gay and lesbian community. From there, you should also visit the **Dr. Kelly McGinnis Library** run by Pink Triangle Services at 251 Bank Street, Suite 301 *(563-3967, pinktriangle.org)*, the largest gay, lesbian, bisexual, and transgender lending library, featuring primarily books with some videos, CDs, and cassettes (membership free! no fees!). For more pride films and magazines, as well as greeting cards, glassware, leather, and novelties, head to **Wilde's** at 367 Bank Street *(234-5512, wildes.com)*.

Chapters

Most locals might not remember the old lunch counter at Woolworths, but that old department store building is now the location of a three-storey **Chapters** megastore *(47 Rideau St., 241-0073)*. Other locations include 2210 Bank Street *(at South Keys, 521-9199)*, 2735 Iris Street *(at Pinecrest Shopping Centre, 596-3003)* and 400 Earl Grey Drive *(271-7553)*. chapters.indigo.ca

Collected Works Bookstore and Coffeebar

Located in the Westboro/Parkdale area, this friendly bookstore has a good-sized kids' section, sale items, and a wide array of titles, as well as coffee and snacks for sale. They feature occasional writing workshops and book launches. *1242 Wellington St. W., 722 1265, collectedworks.com*

Photo: Charles Earl

EXILE Info-shop

Called "Ottawa's first anarchist bookstore," the EXILE Info-shop opened in 2007. The store features alternative and anarchist books and other merchandise not otherwise available in typical bookstores. Run by a collective, the store is open from Wednesday to Sunday, noon to 8 p.m. *256 Bank St. (upstairs), 237-9270, exilebooks.org*

Mother Tongue Books

Owned and operated by the former staff of the late Ottawa Women's Bookstore on Elgin Street from the 1990s, this bookstore is easily the friendliest in town, operating just south of Lansdowne Park in Old Ottawa South. Predominantly a women-oriented store, it also carries a fine selection of LGBTQ titles, Carleton University course books, and one of the most comprehensive local author sections (including poetry) in the city. *1067 Bank St., 730-2346*

Octopus Books

In business for over 30 years, Octopus is one of Canada's first alternative bookstores (it even published an underground newspaper for several years). It was originally established as a socialist/feminist collective (which for years, unfortunately, was run by a board made up entirely of men), and eventually sold as a business in 1997. Still, it's the best place in town to get any sort of social and/or political literature. *116 Third Ave., 233-2589, octopusbooks.org*

Nicholas Hoare Booksellers

This shop, which caters mostly to the bestsellers and children's book crowd, is always a popular stop for tourists. Plus, they host a number of launches throughout the year. *419 Sussex Dr., 562-2665, nicholashoare.com*

Prime Crime Books

Ottawa's mystery bookstore, where you can find anything and everything crime related that's fit to print. Come here to confirm if the butler did, indeed, do it. *891 Bank St., 238 2583, primecrimebooks.com*

FOR THE FAB CROWD

Check out Bob Cabana's **Fab Gear 64** (1964 being the year that the Beatles landed in New York City) in Westboro *(420 Richmond Rd., 725-1964)*. He also showcases and sells a fabulous collection of rock 'n' roll memorabilia, from Beatles dolls to an autographed Rolling Stones poster. Offering one of the finest assortments of pop culture artifacts, the store features a wide selection of vinyl records, *Corner Gas* hockey jerseys, authentic Rockmount Ranch Wear shirts, Hawaiian shirts, and western gear. Not only that, they also have a sandwich and juice bar.

TOGS FOR TOTS

Since the young 'uns grow out of everything so fast anyway, why not shop at **Boomerang Kids Consignment Shop Inc**. in its two locations *(1056 Bank St., 730-0711; 261 Richmond Rd., 722-6671)*, or **Three Bags Full Consignment Shop** *(501 Hazeldean Rd., 836-7621)*. Both businesses also have a selection of maternity clothes. For new wee apparel, check out **Glebe Side Kids** *(793 Bank St., 235-6552)* or **West End Kids** *(373 Richmond Rd., 722-8947, westendkids.ca)*.

Shirley Leishman Books

Ottawa's west-end independent bookseller, this store's small space has hosted some of the largest **Harry Potter** launches in town.
Westgate Shopping Centre, 1309 Carling Ave., 722-8313

Venus Envy

Ottawa's own store (a second location for a business that started in Halifax, Nova Scotia) for "women and the people who love them," Venus Envy is a book, health, and sex store; it also hosts occasional poetry/fiction readings. The Venus Envy stores pride themselves on being a source of quality information (for that burning question you've always been meaning to ask).
320 Lisgar St., 789-4646, venusenvy.ca

Take a Second Look

For used or remaindered books, check out:

Argosy Books: Have a look at their wall of paperback Penguin Classics *(209 Dalhousie St., 241-1319, argosybooks.ca)*.

All Books: Provides a wide range of paperbacks and remainders; a great place to find a good gumshoe story to read while waiting in line for a film at the ByTowne Cinema next door *(327 Rideau St., 789-9544)*.

Benjamin Books: Perhaps the best place in the city for discounted books from American and Canadian university presses *(three locations, including the original store at 122 Osgoode St., 232-7495; Rideau Centre, 241-0617; 1200 St. Laurent Blvd., 741-9317)*.

Book Bazaar: High-end antiquarian titles as well as more popular editions of what the university student (and beyond) should be reading; also a wide selection of history and literary titles *(417 Bank St., 233-4380, bookbazaar.ca)*.

Book Market: The main three-storey store is at 374 Dalhousie Street *(241-1753)*, with two other locations at Alta Bank Shopping Plaza *(526-3277)* and 1534 Merivale Road *(Nepean, 226-3672)*. This is perhaps the best bookstore in the city for its massive selection of second-hand paperbacks and other more popular titles, including a whole slew of mystery titles, romance novels, and university texts. *bookmarket.ca*

Bytown Bookshop: A small store, but behind all

VINTAGE THREADS

For good secondhand anything, you can't go wrong with the old standards, whether **Value Village** *(1375 Clyde Ave., 288-1390; 1162 Cyrville Rd., 749-4977; 1824 Bank St., 526-5551)*, the **Salvation Army** *(1558 Merivale Rd., 225-4521; 1156 Wellington St. W., 722-8025)* or **St. Vincent de Paul** *(1273 Wellington St. W., 722-7166)*. Some high quality finds (including a selection of women's gloves and men's hats and ties, in case you need to "party like it's 1899") can be picked up at Ottawa's infamous **Ragtime Vintage Clothing** *(43 Flora St., 233-6940)*. It might even be the only place in town to actually find a waistcoat.

the paperbacks, the owner also has a selection of letterpress books, chapbooks and broadsides, including locally published ones *(21 Arlington Ave., 233-2715, bytownbookshop.ca).*

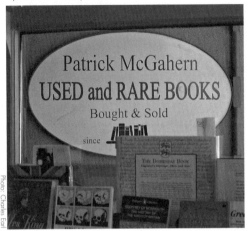

Photo: Charles Earl

Patrick McGahern Books Inc.: This is where the late poet John Newlove used to shop, which by itself suggests McGahern might have some of the best selection of obscure history titles in Ottawa *(783 Bank St., 233-2275, mcgahernbooks.ca).*

Mostly Mags

Photo: Charles Earl

Whether looking for the latest fashion magazine or a copy of the *Ottawa Citizen,* the best repository of small and large periodicals (including foreign and foreign-language) is **Mags & Fags** *(254 Elgin St., 233-9651).* Where else in the city could you pick up a copy of *Brick: A Literary Journal, Hip Hop Weekly, Skeptical Inquirer, Gibbons Stamp Monthly,* and *Cat Fancy,* along with Ottawa's own parliamentary-satire *Frank* magazine? Other good stores include **Britton's Westboro** *(352 Richmond Rd., 729-0551),*

TIMELESS TREASURES

For something unique and utterly charming, go to **Aunt Olive's Vintage Clothing Café** *(209 Gilmour St. at Elgin, 565-0564).* Founded and operated by mother, cook, waitress, and seamstress Jamie Garner, Aunt Olive's exists as a combination thrift shop, café, clothing store, and just about anything else you can imagine. It's a magnificent accident in the middle of Centretown, with little more than word-of-mouth to keep it thriving. Just look for the panties on the front door. There's even a Facebook profile dedicated to the store.

Globe Mags and Cigars *(57 William St., 241-7274)*, New Edinburgh News Stand *(9 Beechwood Ave., 746-8870)* and **Maison de la Presse Bank Street** *(92 Bank St., 230-9774)*. In the centre of the Glebe 'hood, Britton's Glebe *(237-6116)* at 846 Bank Street since 1966, packs into its small location a variety of smoking supplies, magazines, international newspapers, and books, including local interest titles.

Comics, Etc.

The best place in town to shop for comics is **Silver Snail Comics** *(391 Bank St., 232-2609, silversnail.com)*, with the largest selection of new and back issues in the city. A close second goes to the **Comic Book Shoppe** *(thecomicbookshoppe.com)*, with its two locations at 1400 Clyde Avenue *(228-8386)* and 228 Bank Street *(594-3042)*. The Shoppe is also home to much more: gaming, T-shirts, and toys, as well as a large selection of video rentals, including anime. If you can't get that far downtown, you can always check out new and back issues at **Cave Comics** *(134–2446 Bank St., 739-7831)*. For more subversive and underground literature (as well as a slew of hemp products and information), check out Mike's counterculture variety store **Crosstown Traffic** *(593C Bank St., 234-1210; 396 Athlone Ave., 728-4800; crosstowntraffic.ca)*. The best of art, sex, and drugs, it carries the old standards, such as the works of Robert Crumb, and it even has a hardcover *Playboy* edition of *Little Annie Fanny*, signed by Hugh Hefner himself.

Stamps of Approval

In search of a few unique stamps for your collection? Check out **Ian Kimmerly Stamps** *(62 Sparks St., 235-9119, iankimmerly.com)*, located in the historic Bank of Commerce building (see p. 23). If you want to find out anything about stamps, Kimmerly is your man. He had a newspaper column for nearly 20 years, first in the *Ottawa Citizen*, and later in *The Globe and Mail*.

For collectibles for kids, big and little, check out

Game Breakers Sports Cards (*780 Baseline Rd., 228-9554*), or **The Hobby Centre** (134-2446 Bank St., 739-9020), and **Hobby House** (*80 Montreal Rd., 749-5245, hobbyhouse.ca*), both of which are endorsed by the Canadian Association of Railway Modellers (*caorm.org/Pages/hobbyshop.html*).

Photo: Daniel Boulet

Food, Glorious Food

If you'd like to add a little Italian flair to your dinner party, be sure to get to Little Italy's **Luciano's Fine Prepared Foods** (160 Preston St., 236-7545). With friendly service and the absolute best Italian products, including fresh pastas, cheeses, and meats, it's the ultimate in old-fashioned Italian delicacies. For the best of new-world Italian, check out **La Bottega Nicastro Fine Food Shop** in the Byward Market (*64 George St., 789-7575*) or **Nicastro's Italian Food Emporium** (*1558 Merivale Rd., 225-3470*). For other fresh specialty foods, there's also **Boushey's Food Mart** (*348 Elgin St., 236-4482*), with hot lunches and fresh salads as well as groceries; family-owned and operated for six decades.

Other delicious options include **Gourmet Canada** (*176 Beechwood Ave., 746-4515*), with a huge selection of foods from across Canada and around the globe, including Okanagan Valley fruit preserves, wild rice and spices from Manitoba, jalapeño jellies from Alberta, Niagara Peninsula jams and preserves, Arctic char, pickled garlic from Ontario, apple butter and pumpkin jams from Nova Scotia, and pickled fiddleheads and cattails from Quebec and New Brunswick. Or check out **Thyme and Again Creative Catering and Take Home Food**, providing an array of holiday/monthly menus, where you can take your food with you, or just sit by the window with a cup of tea, coffee, or hot cider (*1255 Wellington St. W., 722-0093, thymeandagaincatering.com*).

LOOT!

For years I joked that Ottawa didn't have looters because all of our good stores were too far apart; unfortunately, the colossal blackout of 2003 that took out most of the eastern seaboard in Canada and the United States proved me wrong. Sadly, some of the rare reports of riots and looting in affected areas came from Ottawa's own west end, mainly along Merivale Road. On the first night of the Ottawa blackout, for example, there were 22 incidents of looting and three serious house fires, including one that took the life of a 15-year-old boy. Certainly nothing to be proud of; it's also a terrible thing to have to hear about from David Letterman or Conan O'Brien, both of whom made jokes about Ottawa in their broadcasts at the time.

Photo: John W. MacDonald

PREMIUM PRODUCE

For fresh fruits and vegetables, we'd recommend either location of the **Herb and Spice Shop** (*1310 Wellington St. W., 722-5747; 375 Bank St., 232-4087*), or the **Natural Food Pantry** in Westgate Mall (*1309 Carling Ave., 728-1255, naturalfoodpantry.com*) for any and all of your bulk or specialty food needs.

Deli-icious

If a deli is more your style, head to the **Ottawa Bagelshop and Deli** (1321 Wellington St. W., 722-8753, bagelshop.ca), which offers a variety of bagels (including kosher) made on-site, as well as hot meals, salads, or whatever else you might desire for lunch. You could also try the little deli inside the **Place Bell Mall** (160 Elgin St.), where you can mix with the government rank and file if you go during lunch. Adam Przystal has been making sausages for over 25 years; try them at **Adam's Sausages & Meat Products** (1427 Michael St., 749-3336, adamssausages.com). The lunch counter at **Sausage Kitchen Fine Sausages & Meats** (5 Byward Market Square, 241-6358) is usually packed, so be prepared for a line-up. But as one of the few places in town to get items like game birds and venison, it's worth it.

Photograph of Adam's Sausages & Meat Products, by Lois Siegel

Our Daily Bread

For the best in baked goods around the city, I recommend either location of **Rideau Bakery** (384 Rideau St., 789-1019; 1666 Bank St., 737-3355), for their selection of breads (including authentic European rye), cakes, pastries, and other products (and they still make their own icing). The focus is firmly on baked goods, not décor, so don't be thrown by the time-warp feel of the original Rideau Street location's 1930s chrome and powder-blue stools along a silver coffee bar, or its orange walls. A documentary was made about the bakeries' owners, the Kardish family, entitled *One of the Last* (2007), produced and directed by Ottawa filmmaker Ed Kucerak. In both English and Hebrew, the film includes the story of the family's beginnings in the Ukraine over a century ago.

Alternatively, head to the **Middle East Bakery** *(605 Somerset St. W., 238-7342)*, where you can sometimes catch a view of the freshest pita bread in town (regular and whole wheat) coming straight out of the oven (in winter, this is a good place to walk by and catch a gust of hot bread air).

Photo: Serge Brousseau

Sweet Stuff

If you need a sugar fix, get yourself to any of the funky Ottawa locations of the Toronto-based **Sugar Mountain** *(sugarmountain.ca)*. Filled with tubs of candy, sweets, and other desirables, the stores also have loads of kitschy 1950s and 60s memorabilia for sale and on display, including album covers, lunchboxes, and other items adorned with the likes of Elvis Presley, Marilyn Monroe, and the Ramones. How could you go wrong? Locations include 753 Bank Street *(787-5775)*, 286 Elgin Street *(230-8886)*, and 71 William Street *(789-8428)*. At the William Street location, you can also buy ice cream. But, if you want ice cream without the Joey Ramone, be sure to get over to **Purple Cow Fudge & Candy Co**. at 798 Bank Street *(236-1095)*. For a simple chocolate high, check out **Rocky Mountain Chocolate Factory** at 55 Byward Market Square *(241-1091, rockychoc.com)* or **Godiva Chocolatier Inc**. at 50 Rideau Street *(234-4470)*. For something a little more exotic, check out the Ottawa location of **Stubbe Chocolates** *(375 Dalhousie St., 241-1040, stubbechocolates.com)*. A sister store to the Toronto location, they're part of a family business

BONNY FASHIONS

If you've been invited to a Scottish dance and you haven't a thing to wear, check out the kilts and tartans at **McCarthy Highland Services** *(61 Borealis Cres., 291-2841, mccarthyhighland.com)*, **The Scottish Lion** in Maxville *(an hour's drive west along Hwy. 417, 1-800-956-5458)*, or **Kijiji Ottawa** *(355 Gilmour St., 238-2058)*. Kijiji is the only place in the region with its own extensive in-house line of Scottish attire and full regalia direct from Scotland.

FOR KIDS OF ALL AGES

The store for kids of all ages, **Mrs. Tiggy Winkle's** *(a name inspired by a Beatrix Potter book)* has five locations in Ottawa, and we recommend them all: 809 Bank Street in the Glebe *(234-3836)*, the Rideau Centre *(50 Rideau St., 230-8081)*, the Bayshore Shopping Centre *(100 Bayshore Dr., 721-0549)*, the Place D'Orléans Mall *(off Hwy. 17, in Orléans, 834-8988)* and 317 Richmond Road *(761-6055)*. No matter how old or how grumpy you think you are, you would be hard pressed to walk out of here without purchasing *something*. *mrstiggywinkles.ca*

One of the sweetest things you can do for yourself (or someone else) is place an order with **The Girl with the Most Cake** *(839-2741, thegirlwiththemostcake.com)* for beautiful designer cakes. Owner-operator Linda Bartlett doesn't have a storefront, but if you check out her website, you can get a glimpse of her creations that are almost too beautiful to eat. Promotional materials for her business include a fun series of collectible trading cards. If that isn't your style, there's always the slightly less quirky but equally mouthwatering **Artistic Cake Design** at 1390 Clyde Avenue *(722-4801, artisticcakedesign.ca)*, **Cakes by Tatiana** at 1202 Bank Street *(523-2112, cakesbytatiana.com)* or **Pasticceria Gelateria Italiana** at 200 Preston Street *(233-2104, pasticceria.ca)*.

Cake by Tatiana, cakesbytatiana.com, photograph by Lois Siegel

started in the northern German city of Meppen in 1845 by Johann Heinrich Petrus Stubbe, and brought to Canada by a more recent Stubbe, Heinrich Johann, who operates the two stores with his son Daniel. Today, the two locations provide the finest in European chocolates, including an array of hand-dipped truffles made daily. Or, if you want that good ol' Canadian maple sugar rush, get thee immediately to **Heritage Maple Product** at 55 Byward Market Square *(241-3875)*.

24-Hour Shopping

Since Ottawa has a higher percentage of a white-collar working population (Gatineau has the factories and Ottawa has the Parliament Buildings), there aren't a whole lot of shift workers, translating into very little need for after-hours shopping. Nevertheless, there are a few, such as various locations of the **Loeb** chain of grocery stores, including 2636 Innes Road *(837-1845)* and 1930 Montreal Road *(744-2961)* in Gloucester, 1675 10th Line Road, C1 *(837-2614)* in Orléans, 345 Carleton Avenue *(725-3065)* and 245 Rideau Street *(241-9331)* further downtown, 2515 Bank Street *(731-7410)* at Southgate, and 250 Greenbank Road (828-9321) and 1360 Richmond Road (828-4207) in the west end. Otherwise, the **Shoppers Drug Mart** in the Rideau Centre *(236-2533)* stays open the latest, closing at 11 p.m. from Monday to Friday, and 9 p.m. on Saturday and Sunday.

For years now, Ottawa has managed to create its own unique neighbourhoods of musicians, actors, and other entertainers, as well as invent its our own version of "Hollywood North," producing and playing host to award-winning actors and other stars. Also, only in a city like Ottawa could entertainment oddities originate in such droves, from the pop-punk stylings of Furnaceface, the antics of comedian Tom Green, the hidden secrets of Crawley Films, or the B-movie greatness of *Jesus Christ, Vampire Hunter* (2001).

You Oughta Know Her

Reinvesting the money she made as a child actor on *You Can't Do That on Television* (see p. 120), **Alanis Morissette** recorded and released an independent single, "Fate Stay with Me," in 1986. Billed simply as "Alanis," she spent the rest of the 80s striving to become Canada's pop queen (a northern equivalent of Debbie Gibson or Tiffany). She released the dance-pop confection *Alanis* (1991) and the more ballad-driven *Now Is the Time* (1992). A year later, she moved to Los Angeles and made a very drastic sound and image overhaul, becoming an angry yet self-possessed, post-grunge diva. In 1995, she released *Jagged Little Pill* on Madonna's Maverick Records, featuring the hit single "You Oughta Know," selling 30 million copies around the world, making it, at the time, the highest-selling album by a female artist and third highest-selling album ever. Since then, she released *Supposed Former Infatuation Junkie* (1998), *Under Rug Swept* (2001), *So-Called Chaos* (2004), *Alanis Morissette: The Collection* (2005), and a 10th-anniversary acoustic version of *Jagged Little Pill* (2005).

Alanis was born in 1974 at Ottawa's Riverside Hospital, 12 minutes after her twin brother, Wade. She attended Glebe Collegiate Institute, where one of her gold records appears on the wall of the school office, donated as a thank you to the school for supporting her career. Morissette has homes in Los Angeles and Vancouver, but still keeps an apartment in Ottawa. The Mayor of Ottawa named March 8, 1996, "Alanis Morissette Day."

Canada's Film Pioneer

Before the National Film Board of Canada existed, there was Ottawa's **Crawley Films**, founded in 1939 by Frank Radford "Budge" Crawley and his first wife, Judith Rosemary Sparks Crawley. Called "an audacious rogue," a trail-blazing entrepreneur, and a true pioneer in Canadian film, Frank Crawley is often considered Canada's answer to American filmmakers Jack Warner or Sam Goldwyn. First housed in the abandoned St Matthias Church Hall at 19 Fairmont Avenue in the Hintonburg area (in the 1930s, the church itself moved to its new location at 555 Parkdale Ave.), the company was founded not just to make films, but also to build a film *industry*. With the head office in Ottawa and branch offices in Toronto and Montreal, this husband-and-wife team made Crawley Films into Canada's largest independent film company, and the most successful of its kind in North America, rivaling the National Film Board in production of sponsored films. In the 43 years of Crawley Films' existence, it produced more than 5,000 films – including industrial shorts, features, documentaries, animation, television programs, and commercials – and won 255 international awards. Not only a business partner, Judith Crawley was also an accomplished director, writer, editor, producer, camera operator, sound recorder, and actress, working directly on numerous Crawley Films projects and winning awards, later serving as president of the Canadian Film Institute from 1979 to 1982. Their first film together, *L'Ile d'Orléans* (1938), was made during their honeymoon, and won the Hiram Percy Maxim Award for Best Amateur Film. They went on to produce such films as *The Loon's Necklace* (1948), *Newfoundland Scene* (1950), *Amanita Pestilens* (1962), *The Man Who Skied Down Everest* (1975), *Hamlet* (1973), and *The Luck of Ginger Coffey* (1964) (from the Brian Moore novel), as well as one of the first animated series for television, *The Tales of the Wizard of Oz* (1962). Crawley Films were innovators: they produced the first Canadian feature filmed in colour, the first shot simultaneously in English and French, the first in Canada to utilize 16mm synchronized sound, and the first Canadian feature to win an Academy Award (for the documentary *The Man Who Skied Down Everest*). Some of the people who worked with Crawley early in their careers include director Irvin Kershner, British thespian Robert Shaw, Christopher Plummer, Lorne Greene,

Photo: John W. MacDonald

OUR CANADIAN IDOL

Born Ava Gougeon-Avila in Ottawa in 1987 and raised in Gatineau, **Eva Avila** was the winner on the fourth season of CTV's *Canadian Idol* in 2006. A former winner of the province-wide singing competition "Jeune Diva du Quebec," Avila first sang in public at the age of two, busked with her father when she was three, and was a winner on CJOH-TV's *Homegrown Café* at the age of nine. She is only the second singer from Quebec to crack *Canadian Idol's* top 10, and first to win the event. Just days after the release of her 2006 debut album, *Somewhere Else*, she performed the national anthem at the 94th Grey Cup game in Winnipeg.

animator Bill Mason, and documentarian Pierre Perrault.

The company was eventually bought out in 1982 by former employee Bill Stevens of Atkinson Film Arts. Unfortunately, by 1989, Atkinson Film Arts announced on the 50th anniversary of the founding of Crawley Films that all the old Crawley Studios and facilities would be sold (the old building is still there, across from the big church on Wellington Street West, a shadow of its former self). Through advents in computer technology, Stevens managed to downsize from a fully equipped 30,000-square-foot (9144-sq-m) production studio to a home computer. In August 2006, he became general manager of CHRI 99.1 FM, Ottawa's only Christian radio station, and the company that produced various animated series over the past 20 years including *The Adventures of Teddy Ruxpin*, *Babar*, *Care Bears*, *The Raccoons*, and *Curious George* has been put on the backburner somewhat, now run by Stevens' wife and son.

They Came From Ottawa (or at Least, Were Raised Here)

There are notable people that have actually been born and raised in Ottawa, and who return every so often – really, it's true. Here are some you might have heard of:

Dan Aykroyd: An actor and comedian, best known perhaps as "Elwood Blues" from *The Blues Brothers* (1980), Aykroyd, who was born in Ottawa, started his acting career at Ottawa's Carleton University with Sock 'n' Buskin, the campus theatre/drama club. He dropped out to work with Second City Stage Troupe in Toronto. At one point, Carleton wanted to name a building after him, but they were soon told that they couldn't name a

building after a student who didn't actually graduate. They settled by awarding him an honorary doctorate in 1994, in a media frenzy that included Aykroyd arriving on campus on a motorcycle, with then-Heritage Minister Sheila Copps along for the ride. Ever the humble and approachable Canadian boy, you can still see Aykroyd around town, with friends at any number of places in the Byward Market.

Maria del Mar del Castillo: Better known as **Maria del Mar**, this actress was born in Madrid in 1964 (the youngest of six children), debuted in the long-running 1980s TV drama series *Street Legal*, and has since appeared in a number of other projects including *TekWar* (1994), *Relativity* (1996), and *Blue Murder* (2001). Not to be confused with *another* Maria del Mar, the lead singer of Canadian 80s goth band National Velvet.

Ted Follows: Born in Ottawa in 1926, Follows has had numerous TV and film appearances, including *Rob Roy, the Highland Rogue* (1954), *McQueen* (TV series, 1969), *Paperback Hero* (1973), *Cold Comfort* (1989), *Wojeck: Out of the Fire* (1992), and *J. F. K.: Reckless Youth* (1993). Despite his long resumé, he's probably best known as the father of actress Megan Follows, who played the title role in the CBC's *Anne of Green Gables* TV movies.

Luba Goy: One of the writers/performers with CBC's *The Royal Canadian Air Farce*, Goy was raised in Ottawa and attended the Glebe Collegiate Institute. She has received many honours, including the Governor General's Performing Arts Award, a Juno, Maclean's Honour Roll, a star on "Canada's Walk of Fame" in Toronto, and two honorary doctorate degrees. Says Luba: "Mama is so proud [of my acting], she tells everyone: 'Luba barely finished high school, but she's [already] a doctor!'"

TAKING IT BY THE BULLHORN

When talking about music in Ottawa, it's nearly impossible not to mention **Little Bullhorn Productions**. Tucked behind Pubwells at a dead-end off Preston Street in Little Italy, music producer Dave Draves' in-house studio has produced more local music by young bands and artists than almost anyone in Ottawa. Open since 2000, the studio has recorded the likes of Jim Bryson, Julie Doiron, Kathleen Edwards, Sue Foley, Greenfield Main, The John Henrys, Alex Mortimer, The Recoilers, the Spiny Anteaters, Skydiggers, Stand GT, Snailhouse, and the Wooden Stars. *magma.ca/~draves*

SIX DEGREES OF LORNE GREENE

A graduate of Ottawa's Lisgar Collegiate High School, **Lorne Greene** went on to a long and varied acting career featuring dozens of television and film appearances. Depending on how old you are, he is best remembered either as Ben Cartwright in the 1960s TV Western *Bonanza*, as Commander Adama in the 70s sci-fi series *Battlestar Galactica*, or for the 80s nature series *Lorne Greene's New Wilderness*. His daughter, Gillian Greene, is married to director Sam Raimi, who directed *Superman Returns* (2006) (he can be forgiven for this, given his work on the *Spider-Man* franchise); one of the creators of the comic-book hero Superman, Canadian Joe Shuster, was first cousin to Toronto's Frank Shuster, of Wayne & Shuster fame. Frank's daughter, Rosie, was the first wife of another Canadian-born Lorne: Lorne Michaels, creator of *Saturday Night Live*.

Jessica Holmes: This alumna of Ottawa's Canterbury High School and the Canadian Improv Games graduated from the Radio & Television Arts program at Ryerson University. She briefly had her own TV show, *The Holmes Show* (2002), and now appears regularly on *The Royal Canadian Air Farce*.

Rich Little: This graduate of Lisgar Collegiate was the oldest of three boys, two of whom ended up using their voices for a living (another brother did children's puppet shows for years). Little rose to prominence in the 1960s and 70s on such American shows as *The Ed Sullivan Show* and *The Tonight Show* with his impressions of actors, presidents, and other personalities. These days, he can be seen regularly in such places as Las Vegas, where he still performs for crowds of people whose parents might have thought him the cleverest guy around.

Les Lye and Bill Luxton: Anyone who grew up in the Ottawa Valley during the 1960s, 70s, and 80s will remember CJOH's *Uncle Willy & Floyd* show, which featured strange sketches and guest appearances by Bruno Gerussi, Margaret Trudeau, and Alanis Morissette. Lye and Luxton worked for decades producing Saturday morning television, and Lye was instrumental as part of *You Can't Do That On Television* (see p.120). In 2003, the two were honoured with lifetime achievement awards from the Alliance of Canadian Cinema, Television and Radio Artists for their work.

Mark McKinney: One of the Toronto comedy troupe *The Kids in the Hall,* McKinney also spent a season on *Saturday Night Live* (apparently all five were offered spots, but only McKinney accepted). A true local boy, he even made reference to his upbringing in a *Kids* sketch, dropping out of his blues man character to say, "I can't do the hambone — I'm from the Ottawa-Hull area!" He has appeared in a number of productions since, including theatre, film, and the CBC-TV series *Slings & Arrows* (2003–06), and irregularly on Aaron Sorkin's *Studio 60 on the Sunset Strip* (2006–07) with Ottawa-raised Matthew Perry.

Matthew Perry: Born in Williamstown, Massachusetts, and best known for the TV sitcom *Friends* and the short-lived *Studio 60 on the Sunset Strip* (brilliant but somehow unwatched), Perry was raised in Ottawa, where he became a top-ranked junior tennis player. His mother, Suzanne Perry Morrison, was a press aide for Prime Minister Pierre Trudeau (she now lives in Toronto with her second husband, the former CTV anchorman

Keith Morrison). Perry attended Ashbury College while in Ottawa. After moving to Los Angeles at 15 to live with his father, the actor John Bennett Perry, young Matt became more interested in acting, and put his career in tennis behind him. He returns to the city regularly to, among other things, attend Senators playoff games.

Kelly Rowan: Born in Ottawa in 1967, but raised in Toronto, Rowan has appeared in dozens of films and TV shows, including *Street Legal*, *DaVinci's Inquest*, *CSI: Crime Scene Investigation*, and *The O.C.*

Sonja Smits: Born on a dairy farm in the Ottawa Valley, actress Smits seems to pop up in just about every production on Canadian TV, including *Street Legal* (1986–92), *The Diviners* (1993), *TekWar* (1994), *Traders* (1996–2000), *The Eleventh Hour* (2002–05), and *The Atwood Stories* (2002).

Just Passing Through

Called a city of transients by some, Ottawa has been home (at least temporarily) to a number of peripatetic people. Here is but a short list of some celebrity transients:

Adam Beach: A Canadian actor fast gaining a reputation at home and abroad, Adam Beach was born in Ashern, Manitoba in 1972. Beach is of Salteaux descent, and spent his first eight years on the Dog Creek Indian Reserve before moving to Winnipeg, then settling in Ottawa as an adult. He has worked with productions at the Ottawa Little Theatre and the Independent Filmmakers Co-Operative of Ottawa. He has had notable movie roles in, among others, *Dance Me Outside* (1995), *The Rez* (1996), *Smoke Signals* (1998), *Windtalkers* (2002), and Clint Eastwood's *Flags of Our Fathers* (2006). He currently has a recurring role in TV's *Law & Order: Special Victims Unit*.

MADE IN OTTAWA

Here are some feature films, TV movies, and miniseries that were shot in the capital region, and their starring actors:

Captains of the Clouds (1942), James Cagney

The Luck of Ginger Coffey (1964), Robert Shaw

Threshold (1981), Donald Sutherland

Mr. and Mrs. Bridge (1990), Paul Newman

Descending Angel (1990), George C. Scott

Batman and Robin (1997), George Clooney

Two's a Mob (1998), Lorraine Ansell

Grey Owl (1999), Pierce Brosnan

House of Luk (2001), Michael Moriarty

Trudeau (2002), Colm Feore

Tom Cruise: Believe it or not, Thomas Cruise Mapother IV (the actual name on his birth certificate) spent part of his formative years in Ottawa (as well as many other places) due to the fact that his father kept moving the family around.

Brendan Fraser: The son of a Canadian travel executive who frequently moved his family, Fraser, the star of *The Mummy, Dudley Do-Right, Bedazzled,* and *The Mummy Returns,* lived in various cities while growing up, including Ottawa.

Matt Frewer: Don't recognize the name? Well, if you're old enough, the name of his alter ego may ring a bell: Max Headroom. The Canadian actor played the 1980s cyber-icon in both a British TV series and (more famously) in Coca-cola commercials (see photo). Frewer went on to appear in both film and TV in the UK *(Monty Python's The Meaning of Life)*, the US *(PSI Factor)* and Canada *(DaVinci's Inquest* and currently, CBC's *Intelligence)*. Raised predominantly in Victoria, BC, and Ottawa, he was quarterback on his high school football team in Peterborough, but a serious hockey injury at the age of 16 sidelined his hopes for a sports career. After living a decade in the UK and then in the US as an adult, he moved his family to the Gatineau Hills in the late 90s, so, as he said, his daughter could grow up around trees instead of concrete.

Norm Macdonald: One of the best news anchors on *Saturday Night Live*, Quebec City-born Macdonald lived for a while in Ottawa where he attended Algonquin College's broadcasting and television program (but dropped out). His two brothers, Leslie and Neil, are both newscasters for the CBC. Early on, one of his brothers tried to get him a job as a reporter for an Ottawa newspaper. Norm failed the interview because he didn't have a car. He said he was hoping news would be within walking distance.

Christopher Plummer: the Toronto-born actor, who grew up with his single mother in Montreal, spent a couple of years training for the theatre with the Canadian Repertory Company in Ottawa and, in two short years there, played 75 different roles. He's probably best known for his starring role opposite Julie Andrews in *The Sound of Music* (1965). His mother, Isabella Mary Plummer, was granddaughter of Sir John Abbott, third Prime Minister of Canada.

It Came from Nepean

When so many talented people come out of a particular area in a city, you have to start asking questions about what's in that region's water supply. Much like Toronto's Scarborough, which spawned such folk as Mike Myers, Phil Hartman, and the Barenaked Ladies, the City of Nepean (since amalgamated into Ottawa) is somehow responsible for a number of Ottawa's own unique talents.

Tom Green: He may not have been his best in *Freddy Got Fingered* (2001) or as "The Chad" in *Charlie's Angels* (2000), but who can resist the Tom Green of *Road Trip* (2000), or any of his episodes of *The Tom Green Show*. The program ran first on Rogers Cable 22 in Ottawa, briefly on the Comedy Network (after a failed courtship by CBC), and then on MTV. He hosted *The Late Show* for a stint when David Letterman was out with shingles. This is also the kid who led the short-lived hip-hop group Organized Rhyme, with their first and only hit "Check the O.R." getting nominated for a Juno Award in 1993.

Greg Lawrence: Born in Belleville, Ontario, Jack of all TV trades Lawrence grew up in Nepean and studied broadcasting at Algonquin College at the same time as future comedian Tom Green. Lawrence has since gone on to write/produce and act in the TV series *Kevin Spencer* (1999–2005), *Butch Patterson: Private Dick* (1999), and *The Endless Grind* (2001).

Sandra Oh: Born to Korean immigrants and raised in Nepean, Oh made a name for herself in 1993 in the made-for-TV film version of Evelyn Lau's memoir, *Runaway: The Diary of a Street Kid*. Oh has appeared in films on both sides of the 49th parallel, including

STATES OF GRACE

While Scotland may have the Loch Ness monster, Ottawa has a mysterious creature of its own. Decked out in a cheap, ill-fitting suit and wrestling mask to obscure his identity, the **Unknown Wrestler** has been making appearances around town the past few years. Armed with his trusty companion Hamburgler, this — for lack of a better phrase — performance artist has graced stages at various Ottawa venues ringing a bell between terrible one-liners (and we mean *terrible*) at the club Zaphod Beeblebrox a few years back. The brainchild of Ottawa actor-comic-musician-bartender **Josh Grace**, the Unknown Wrestler has also been an integral part of a number of Ottawa cult-comedy director Lee Demarbre's film productions (see p.121), including roles such as the Aztek mummy Motecazama, vampire surgeon Dr Pretorious, and the nine-foot Bionic Bigfoot.

Grace first performed around town as Remi Royale in the mid-1990s, supposedly a cheesy French-Canadian rock star in the band Les Tonnes du Fromage; one of their performances included Royale stripping down to a fur jockstrap. Managing to get himself onto *The Price is Right* in the early part of the decade, he told Bob Barker that he was studying "bioscatology" at Carleton University, a word he later said was the "study of shit." If you can imagine it, Grace managed to win the game show's Showcase Showdown, only to blow the proceeds on guitars and parties for his friends, and later toured as a roadie for Ottawa Celtic-punk heroes Jimmy George (see p. 121). Over the past few years, the Unknown Wrestler has been circulating the airwaves of CBC Radio 3.

Last Night (1998), *The Red Violin* (1998), *Long Life, Happiness & Prosperity* (2002), *Under the Tuscan Sun* (2003), and *Sideways* (2004), directed by her then-husband Alexander Payne. She currently stars in the hit TV series *Grey's Anatomy*.

What's Your Major?

Here are a few notable students who attended institutes of higher learning in Ottawa:

Samantha Bee: Born in Toronto, Samantha Bee has been a correspondent for *The Daily Show with Jon Stewart* on Comedy Central since 2003 as the first (and so far only) non-American correspondent, and regularly appears in Canadian-specific spots. She attended the University of Ottawa.

Mary Lou Finlay: A veteran CBC TV and radio host, Finlay co-hosted Radio One's *As It Happens* from 1997 to 2005. She graduated *cum laude* from the University of Ottawa in 1967 with a BA in English and French Literature.

Peter Jennings: Born in Toronto, the precocious Jennings started his broadcast career as the host of a half-hour CBC Radio kids' show called *Peter's People* when he was nine. He attended the University of Ottawa and Carleton University, but dropped out and went to work at a radio station in Brockville, Ontario. After working at other media venues,

including CTV, he went on to become the face of ABC News, delivering the nightly headlines to North Americans for over 20 years. Despite living in the US for much of his adult life, he didn't get his US citizenship until 2003. He died in 2005 from lung cancer at the age of 67.

Alex Trebek: Born Giorgi Suka-Alex Trebek in Sudbury, Ontario, the face of American trivia show *Jeopardy!* (1984–present) started out as host for *Reach for the Top* (1965), and later, *The Wizard of Odds* (1973), produced by Canadian-born Alan Thicke. He graduated from the University of Ottawa with a degree in philosophy.

Put Your Head on His Shoulder

Born and raised in Ottawa, **Paul Anka** first achieved success in the 1950s as a teenage singing star. Unlike many of his heartthrob contemporaries, though, he wrote his own songs. He also wrote the classic tune "My Way," made famous by Frank Sinatra (or Sid Vicious, depending on your tastes). His talents didn't stop there. He later appeared in films, including *The Longest Day* (1962). His first single "Diana" was initially broadcast on Ottawa DJ Gord Atkinson's radio show on CFRA. Atkinson, who had interviewed hundreds of celebrities on his program over the years, including Elvis Presley, Bob Hope, and Bing Crosby, was an Anka supporter from the start. Despite over 100 records to his name, Anka had only one more major hit after 1959: 1974's "(You're) Having My Baby."

Anka played Ottawa every few years from the late 1960s onward to smaller but very appreciative crowds and often harsh reviews; in fact, he was often abused by hometown media throughout the 70s (much as Alanis was years later, proving yet again that Ottawa tends to eat its young). When he performed at the Ex in 1981, his publicity manager suggested that his home city declare August "Paul Anka Month," as well as grant him an "Entertainer of The Decade" award. It all seemed a bit much; the city officials reminded Anka's publicist that they had *already* named a street after him, that he had been made an honourary citizen, and had been given the key to the city in 1972. Instead, they arranged a luncheon recognizing Anka's 25 years in show business, gave him a commemorative medal, and

SATISFACTION AT LAST

The year 2005 was one to remember for fans of the **Rolling Stones** in Ottawa. Not only did their concert at Frank Clair Stadium mark their first appearance in Ottawa since 1965, they also chose Ottawa as the shooting location for their video for "Streets of Love" the following night into the wee wee hours at the music venue Zaphod Beeblebrox. Included in the video were locals picked off the streets. During the time the Stones were in town, St Giles Presbyterian Church posted this on their letter board: "CAN'T GET NO SATISFACTION / TRY JESUS / SATISFACTION GUARANTEED."

made the day of his concert "Paul Anka Day." The show itself drew 8,000, slightly more than half of capacity, and the media, of course, gave him a lacklustre review, even calling him a "lounge lizard." Aside from a private sendoff for Pierre Trudeau in 1984, this was the singer's last public performance in Ottawa for years. But in the early 90s, he was briefly a partial owner of the Ottawa Senators, and was instrumental in getting investors for the renewed Ottawa hockey franchise.

LUCKY RON FOR MAYOR

For more than 20 years, Lucky Ron (a.k.a. Ron Burke) has been playing everything from rockabilly to old-time country tunes as either a solo performer or as part of the "Lucky Ron Show," not to mention appearances with the old western swing band the Black Donnellys. An Ottawa cult favourite, he currently plays a regular Saturday afternoon show at the Chateau Lafayette to packed crowds of rowdies (see p. 127), and has even run for office of Mayor of Ottawa a few times. Chestnuts from his repertoire include "The Battle of New Orleans" and Johnny Cash's "Ring of Fire." If you recognize his wife, Kathleen, it's probably from her own band, The McGillicuddy Sisters.

In June 2007, Canada Post unveiled a series of new stamps to honour Canadian music legends, including Anne Murray, Gordon Lightfoot, Joni Mitchell, and Paul Anka.

Homegrown Talent

Jim Bryson: Former frontman for the band Punchbuggy, Bryson has been producing solo material that has earned him a reputation as Ottawa's own musicians' musician. Not only did Kathleen Edwards (see next page) include a cover version of his song "Somewhere Else" on her second CD, she has also recruited him as part of her touring band. His albums include *Jim Bryson and the Occasionals* (2000), *The North Side Benches Vinyl LP* (2003), *The North Side Benches CD* (2003), and *Where the Bungalows Roam* (2007).

Kathleen Edwards: From pouring coffee at the Starbucks at Elgin Street and Jack Purcell Lane to recording two amazing alt-country albums, Ottawa's Kathleen Edwards has come a long way. She's been the darling of David Letterman and toured with Willie Nelson. Her CDs include *Failer* (2003), *Live from the Bowery Ballroom* (2003), and *Back to Me* (2005). After a few years of touring and time spent living in Toronto, she and her partner have moved to Hamilton, Ontario, but she still makes frequent stops in Ottawa, both on and off stage.

The Fiftymen: Ottawa's preeminent cow-punkers. Frontman Todd Gibbon started his music career as the bass player for **Stand GT**, a Glengarry County chicken-coop band (they didn't have a garage) when the four were in high school together in Alexandria, Ontario, just an hour's drive east of the city (classmates included your humble author), eventually forming his own band, **Crash 13**. Former Stand GT frontman Chris Page (both he and Todd were also briefly in the band Resin Scraper) produced solo work under the name **Glen Nervous** (after someone else's mis-hearing of his hometown, Glen Nevis, in eastern Ontario), and now under his own.

The Five Man Electrical Band: "Sign, sign, everywhere a sign. . . ." Who can forget the hook of this early 70s anti-authoritarian anthem? The Five Man Electrical Band, the group responsible for the song, was originally formed in Ottawa in 1964 as the Staccatos, with members Rick Belanger, Peter Fallis, Brian Rading, and Vern Craig, with Les Emmerson joining the band after Fallis left. Signing with Capitol Records, the Staccatos recorded a string of singles, including "Half Past Midnight," which sold over 25,000 copies in Canada. After a series of disappointments, they re-formed as the Five Man Electrical Band with Emmerson, Rading, Rick and Mike Belanger, and Ted Gerow. They recorded songs like "Moonshine (Friend Of Mine)" (which appeared in the film *The Moonshine War*, starring Alan Alda), "Hello Melinda, Goodbye," and

SLIMED AGAIN!

The children's sketch-comedy show *You Can't Do That On Television* began humbly enough on Ottawa's CJOH in 1979. Featuring musical guests, games, call-in segments, and plenty of slapstick humour, the program became a Saturday morning staple. The cast featured Les Lye, of *Uncle Willy & Floyd* (see p. 113) fame, and a troupe of unknown child actors, one of whom would eventually enjoy a very successful recording career: Alanis Morissette. By 1984, the show's ratings dropped and the program was hardly watched, but American cable network Nickelodeon picked up the show and aired it five times a week, helping it to become its highest rated program. The central and enduring gag on the show was getting "slimed," a slapstick routine in which an unsuspecting victim is hit by a bucket-load of bright, pea-green ooze (actually, a mix of baby shampoo and green Jell-O). Running until 1987, *YCDTOT* briefly returned for two seasons with a new cast for 1989–90. The show has been in continuous reruns since. There have even been two cast reunion shows/conventions, including *SlimeCon* (2002) and *SlimeCon 2004: The Return of the Slime* (2004), to mark the show's 25th anniversary.

Here are a few films that were shot and actually take place in the city:

H20 (2004), TV movie: When Canada's Prime Minister drowns in an apparent boating accident, his son (played by Paul Gross) takes office and is drawn into a deceptive world of power and corruption, and a battle for Canada's most precious resource, water. One error: a bartender is seen wearing a baseball cap in a Royal Canadian Legion Hall, which protocol forbids.

The Iron Curtain (1948) (reissued as *Behind the Iron Curtain*): Starring Dana Andrews and Gene Tierney, this thriller is based on the true story of Soviet file clerk Igor Gouzenko (see p. 137), who stole documents from the Soviet Embassy in Ottawa in 1945 and made them public after learning that atomic secrets were being forwarded to Joseph Stalin through his office.

Jesus Christ Vampire Hunter (2001): It was a moment of civic pride when I realized that Ottawa was big enough to produce a B-film we could call our very own. There's just something heartwarming about the fact that a third of the actors in this film worked at the Dominion Tavern on York Street, and another third were regular customers. Writer/actor **Ian Driscoll** and producer/director

"Signs," which hit it big in both Canada and the United States, but by 1975, troubles within the band finally forced a break. Every few years, though, they resurface to perform here and there. The original line-up played a Canada Day show a few years back on Parliament Hill.

Furnaceface: Ottawa rock quartet Furnaceface managed to swing a deal with Cargo Records in 1991 for their second record, *Just Buy It*. After a few national tours, they were really starting to take off. At the same time, Cargo had the rights to Nirvana's first album, *Bleach*, and MCA, which had the rights to Nirvana's breakthrough album *Nevermind* in Canada, were desperate to purchase the rights to *Bleach*. Cargo said sure, but you have to take our three biggest sellers as well, which included – you guessed it – Furnaceface, a move which suddenly took them from the back rack at (as singer/bassist Tom Stewart describes it) "mom-and-pop record stores to being in the front display of every record store in the country." The band remains occasionally active, but hasn't released an album since 2000.

Jimmy George: Probably best known throughout the 1990s, the six-piece Celtic cult band Jimmy George was one of those bands that, if you were an Ottawa musician, you probably performed with or in at some point during their tenure, whether during their early period as buskers in 1991, or their years' worth of weekly shows at the long-lost Duke of Somerset Pub. Jimmy George brought together the best of energetic live shows, drinking, and Celtic songs (they've been compared to Spirit of the West and Great Big Sea). With George Jennings on bass, Mickey Vallee on accordion, Jeff Kerr on banjo, Joel Carlson on mandolin, Tom Werbowetski on drums, and J. Todd on guitar and vocals, the group ceased to record (after three albums) or play regularly as a group, but they continue to play an annual reunion show in Ottawa to celebrate St Patrick's Day.

Lynn Miles: Considered one of Canada's finest singers/songwriters, Lynn Miles has been compared to Lucinda Williams, Shawn Colvin, and Joni Mitchell. She has performed with Sue Foley, Tom Wilson, Ian LeFeuvre (of the band Starling), Keith Glass (Prairie Oyster), and John Geggiem (Chelsea Bridge), and, while teaching voice at the Ottawa Folklore Centre, had future recording artist Alanis Morissette as a student.

Wigged Out

From her small second-storey studio in the Ottawa suburb of Barrhaven, wigmaker **Donna Gliddon** has created wigs for such productions as *Les Misérables*, *Cats*, and dozens of other productions for the National Arts Centre, the Canadian Opera Company, and the Great Canadian Theatre Company. However, this quiet woman doesn't limit herself to work for the stage. She provided the wig for actor/wrestler Tyler Mane for his performance as Sabretooth in the feature film *X-Men* (2000), and also has a client list that boasts the likes of Hollywood actress Shirley MacLaine and Canadian acting legend Shirley Douglas (Douglas's contracts even stipulate that Gliddon provide her wigs exclusively). Working the past 30 years to create over 1,000 wigs for various clients, many of her techniques have been adopted by nearly every wigmaker in Canada. Before the Saskatchewan native moved here from Manchester, England, various Canadian theatres had to go across the pond to see her directly for wig services, thus providing Gliddon the opening she needed to establish her own one-woman industry.

Lee Demarbre – through a series of films that started with *Harry Knuckles* (1998), and continued with *Harry Knuckles and the Treasure of the Aztek Mummy* (1999), *Vampire Hunter, Harry Knuckles and the Pearl Necklace* (2004), and *Black Kissinger* (2006) – have made this old government town that much more liveable. The films are wonderfully subversive, deliberately campy, and intelligent.

Other performers in Driscoll-Demarbre productions include local alt-country musical legend Lucky Ron and Josh Grace, otherwise known as "The Unknown Wrestler (see p. 116)," and music by The Hammerheads, Furnaceface, and Johnny Vegas. Copies of their films are available for rent at Invisible Cinema *(319 Lisgar St., 237-0769)*, Elgin Street Video *(258 Elgin St., 236-1877)*, and The Comic Book Shoppe *(228 Bank St., 594-3042)*.

Screen Scribe

Riel (1979): A bad TV biopic about Métis leader Louis Riel and the Red River Rebellion, with a variety of standard Canadian actors, including Maury Chaykin (star of 1994's *Whale Music*) and William Shatner, who filmed his cameo during a break while shooting *Star Trek: The Motion Picture* (1979). The film portrays a visit to Ottawa by Riel and his cohort Gabriel Dumont that probably never happened in real life.

Undercover Angel (1999): Most famous, perhaps, for bringing *Baywatch* star Yasmine Bleeth to Ottawa (apparently James Earl Jones was here too, but no one remembers him), this film was also one of over 72 (including short comedies, half-hour television shows, music videos, commercials and features) written by Peterborough-born and Ottawa-raised Bryan Michael Stoller.

After years of living in New York and Los Angeles, former stand-up comic and screen-turned-comics writer **John Rogers** returned to Ottawa in 2007. Born in Worcester, Massachusetts, Rogers studied at McGill University in Montreal, lived in Ottawa for a number of years, and married an Ottawan. Some of his film and TV writing credits include *Transformers* (2007), *The Core* (2003), and, a-hem, *Catwoman* (2004) (note that he was author of the *story*, not the *screenplay*; what he wrote didn't make it to the screen), and episodes of *Jackie Chan Adventures* (of which he was also creator) and *Cosby*, but what really gets people excited is his comic book work. He is co-author (with Keith Giffen) of DC Comics' re-launch of the ongoing *Blue Beetle* series. *kfmonkey.blogspot.com*

Nightlife

Despite the fact that Ottawa has a reputation as a city that essentially shuts down at 10 p.m., there are still plenty of options for having fun or causing a bit of trouble within the city limits. Heck, how's this for a ringing endorsement: Prince of Darkness Ozzy Osbourne once picked Ottawa as the home base for his Canadian tour.

A Place Where You Can Act Up

Opened in 1914 as a vaudeville venue, the Imperial Theatre lasted for more than four decades as one of Ottawa's premier movie cinemas, and was popular enough to be fined $20 for overcrowding in 1938 before it finally closed in 1955. It spent a number of inauspicious intervening years as a furniture warehouse before being restored and renovated in the late 70s as a five-level restaurant and discotheque known as **Barrymore's Music Hall**, named for the famous acting siblings (Lionel, John, and Ethel). According to Barrymore's then owner Bob Werba, "In the 1930s and 40s, the Barrymore family was very popular and were regarded as the first family of theatre." After the disco years, it enjoyed a short stint as a live-music club in the early 80s, even hosting a show by a very young U2 in 1981. It was reopened with the help of Zaphod Beeblebrox owner Eugene Haslam in 1995 (who left in 1999). Things came full circle one New Year's Eve when Ottawa's Tom Green brought his date, Drew Barrymore, to this club named for her family.
323 Bank St., 233-0307, barrymores.on.ca

Meet You at Zaphod's

Since 1989, **Zaphod Beeblebrox**, a plucky club named after the President of the Galaxy from Douglas Adams' *The Hitchhiker's Guide to the Galaxy*, has been an indispensable part of Ottawa nightlife thanks to a mixture of bands, theme nights – Goth, 80s – and the most dangerous drink in the universe, the Pan-Galactic Gargleblaster. The club was opened on Rideau Street by Ottawa music promoter Eugene Haslam, but a little more than a year later, they were evicted to make way for the Bell building and moved to their current York Street location. Zaphod's has hosted some of the biggest and smallest bands around the world including the Proclaimers, the Mighty Mighty Bosstones, Jewel, Alanis Morissette, the Tea Party, Big Sugar, and countless others.
27 York St., 562-1010, zaphodbeeblebrox.com

A Well-Kept Secret

Occupying a space once used by a strip club, the **Babylon Nightclub** has a strangely shaped interior to see live shows (the position of the bar in the centre gives the whole place a horseshoe feel). Nevertheless, there have been some pretty cool acts here over the years, including occasional all-ages shows, offering a variety of music, but mostly alternative and punk. The best thing about this club: for the first year of its existence, it didn't even have a sign to announce itself. Finally, Ottawa was cool enough to have a nightclub that, if you didn't know of it, you didn't belong there.
317 Bank St., 594-0003, babylonclub.ca

Tuneful Taverns

Carleton Tavern

Photo: Charles Earl

Located in the midst of the Parkdale Market, the Carleton Tavern opened in 1934. It's currently run by brothers Simon and Sam Silankey, who were raised along with their siblings next door in a tiny apartment above the **Ugly Club** diner, which they also used to run with their father. For years, the tavern was part of the diner, which served up one of the finest breakfasts around. The Silankeys closed the diner down in 2006, opening up a smaller version inside the tavern itself, where you can still go for your weekend beer and breakfast, if starting early (or finishing late) is your thing. The place features dart tournaments, playoffs on the big screen television, various bands, and even the odd poetry reading. They also host an annual street party, as well as an annual Christmas dinner.
223 Armstrong St., 728-4424

A DAY TRIP AT NIGHT

A 20-minute drive north over the Quebec border (or a steam train ride away, see p. 44), the **Black Sheep Inn** features some of the best quality music in the Ottawa area, featuring a range of musicians both established and on their way up: Emm Gryner, Jim Cuddy, Garnet Rogers, Lynn Miles, Kathleen Edwards, Atomic 7, Jim Bryson, and Tammy Raybould. If you want to know what everyone will be listening to in a year's time, come here. Be sure to check out the **Temperance Restaurant** situated below the club, and then perhaps stay the night in one of their cozy rooms upstairs. Recently, after much demand, the Inn has started a carpool service from downtown Ottawa, so be sure to check the website to make arrangements.
216 River Rd., Wakefield, Quebec, 819-459-3228, theblacksheepinn.com

VIVA JOHNNY VEGAS

Who else could turn a lounge act originally meant as a joke into a career? **Johnny Vegas** has been a fixture on the Ottawa club scene for years; from the Bingo Jet International nights at Zaphod Beeblebrox in the mid-1990s or more recently as "himself" (he's been known to still answer to "JP"), working the DJ angle at Barrymore's 80s nights. Since then, he's turned his own solo show into a regular act, channeling the Rat Pack days of Sammy Davis Jr and old Blue Eyes himself, at places such as Maxwell's Bistro on Elgin Street.

jvegas.com

PUNK OTTAWA

Like any city with a conservative core, Ottawa has been a home for punks for decades. And the punk scene here remains strong — enough so to support its very own website. Launched in 2001, *punkottawa .com* serves as a bulletin board for events listings at venues around town (including all-ages shows). The site is a veritable hub of underground (and above-ground) activity, including tips on the most punk-rock places to rent movies, grab a bite, get a drink, and tons of other stuff.

Chateau Lafayette

A shadow of its former self, the Chateau Lafayette (Ottawa's oldest hotel and bar, having opened in 1849) is old enough that it once had separate entry doors — one for men, and the other side for "ladies and escorts." Sure, the "Laff" has improved in that it's not as dangerous as it once was, but it's also lost some of its original character. One of the few downtown taverns left in the city, this is this place to see Ottawa legend Lucky Ron perform originals and covers every Saturday. If you're *really* down and out, you can still rent one of the furnished rooms upstairs, small enough that you can open the door, turn on the television, and open the refrigerator all from the comfort of your single bed.

42 York St., 241-4747

Dominion Tavern

In a city where change is constant, something to be praised is a good old-fashioned tavern that is able to remain the same. (Ottawa hasn't actually handed out a tavern licence in years — the only way an establishment can sell quarts; the licences no longer exist.) With some of the cheaper beer in town, and irregular punk shows (check the schedule on their website), "The Dom" is a place where you will be assured that when you are inside, you will hear that same Pixies album playing from over a decade earlier, along with some garage/punk and a bit of ska thrown in for good measure. When it's warm enough, check out their back patio, which was once voted "Best Patio" in an *Ottawa X-Press* poll. And if you decide you've had enough of this place, you can either go upstairs to the strip club, or next door to Zaphod Beeblebrox (see p. 125) without having to call for a cab.

33 York St., 241-7706, tavern.ca

Pub Crawl

Manx Pub

Located downstairs at 370 Elgin Street *(231-2070)*, this is one of those friendly neighbourhood pubs you'd love to have close to where you live. Cornering the market on cool, the **Manx Pub** often sees the likes of musicians **Kathleen Edwards**, **Jim Bryson**, or **Danny Michel** on any given night, or **writers Ken Babstock**, **John Metcalf**, or **Michael Winter**. Even the staff is made up of writers and artists, including visual artist Andrew Farrell and poet David O'Meara, who hosts a reading series here on irregular Saturday afternoons. With a fine menu for lunch, weekend brunch, dinner, and appetizers, the Manx also offers a range of beers and scotch, as well as regular art shows and musical entertainment on Monday nights. But get there early, as this small venue fills up pretty quickly.

A Taste of Ireland

Photo: John W. MacDonald

Arthur Hodgins Jr and Peter Ananny opened **Patty's Pub** *(1186 Bank St., 730-2434)*, previously known as the Mayfair Tea Room, in Old Ottawa South in 1974 in order to, among other things, serve Irish stew and feature Gaelic folk singers. With slightly warped hardwood floors and a comfortable atmosphere, the space manages exactly the right combination of Celtic respectability and old-style charm. Given that it was March 1975 before it received its liquor licence, many current patrons of the establishment might be amazed that it lasted as long as it did without one. There is some debate as to whether this was Ottawa's first Irish pub, or if that honour should go to **Molly McGuire's** in the Market *(130 George St., 241-1972)*. Regardless, the city now has almost too many of them, with the **Aulde Dubliner** *(62 William St. 241-0066, auldedubliner.com)*, **Heart & Crown** Irish Village *(67 Clarence St., 562-0674, irishvillage. ca)*, and **Patty Boland's Irish Pub and Carvery** *(101 Clarence St., 789-7822, pattybolands.com)*, just to name a few.

For years, **D'Arcy McGee's** *(44 Sparks St., 230-4433, darcymcgees.ca)* has been a famous Parliamentarian hangout for journalists, staff, and MPs alike. Another part of the tight lid that Prime Minister Stephen Harper's Conservative government has placed on things has been not allowing their interns to drink at D'Arcy McGee's perhaps lest they blurt out state secrets. I've always suspected that Conservatives couldn't hold their liquor as well as the Liberals or the NDP.

If Irish isn't your style but you still want a pint, there's always **Cornerstone Bar & Grill** *(92 Clarence St., 241-6835, cornerstonebarandgrill.ca)*, **Earl of Sussex Pub** *(431 Sussex Dr., 562-5544)*, and **The Arrow & the Loon** *(99 Fifth Ave., 237-0448)*.

Pub Italia

If you're in Corso Italia (Little Italy), check out the centre of all activity: **Pub Italia** *(434½ Preston St., 232-2326, pubitalia.ca)*. "The world's only Italian pub" (so they tell us), it features 165 distinctive beers from around the world (each with its own glass) with 34 taps, as well as food and ground coffee. Sit in the main section, which is their showcase Belgian pub, **The Abbey**, or on the outdoor patio.

Called to the Bar

Here are a few places off that beaten path that are worth dropping into. A charming secret in Little Italy is **Pubwells** *(96 Preston St., 236-1175)*, a quiet working-class bar that features a fine selection of beer and spirits as well as some of the best pizza around, and a good weekend breakfast special. It's my local, so I might be biased, but I doubt it. Another little spot is the **Mad Cow Pub** *(1070 Bank St., 730-1020)* in Old Ottawa South that has musicians performing various country and folk tunes on guitar (and their open-mike Wednesdays offer the usual combination of dreadful and extremely compelling).

Still looking for the drink that once drove European artists mad? Well, your search stops here at the **Absinthe Café Resto Bar** *(1208 Wellington St., 761-1138, absinthecafe.ca)*. The drink of choice for Oscar Wilde, Toulouse-Lautrec, Vincent Van Gogh, Edgar Allen Poe, and Charles Baudelaire, absinthe was banned in France in 1915, but was never outlawed in Canada.

Get Your Swank On

In the heart of the market, the **Empire Grill** *(47 Clarence St., 241-1343, empiregrill.com)* is a good place to spend an afternoon on the patio with martinis, or enjoy some of the finest dining in the city.

Don't let the name fool you. Buttless chaps and thigh-high boots are not required when drinking at **Kinki** *(41 York St., 789-7559, kinki.ca)*. If you can put up with the slightly self-conscious hipness, come check out the impressive Asian-fusion cuisine, including two-for-one sushi during happy hours (3–5 p.m., weekdays), and DJs as well as various live musicians from Wednesday to Saturday nights.

If mixing dining and politics is more your bag, check out **Parliament Pub** *(101 Sparks St., 563-0636, parliamentpub.com)*, directly across from the Hill.

Lounging Around

If you want to enjoy a martini while listening to a live DJ, the best and coolest place for both is at the **Mercury Lounge**, *(56 Byward Market, upstairs, 789-5324, mercurylounge.net)*. Or check out the **Foundation** *(18B York St., 562-9331, foundationrestaurant.com)*, in one of

spins & needles
craft + DJ night

A CRAFTY NIGHT OUT

If you want to enjoy a martini while listening to a live DJ *and* doing crafts, the best and coolest place for both is at a **spins + needles** night. Hosted at various bars, galleries, legions, or your own private party, Melanie Yugo (crafter/designer) and Jason Pelletier (DJ) offer funky DIY crafts while a perfect beat spins for knit one, purl two. A small cover charge includes materials and instructions. *spinsandneedles.com*

MIDNIGHT MUNCHIES

Once you've exhausted yourself from taking in too much loud music and drink, stop in at one of various late-night establishments, whether it be Vietnamese soup at the late-night **Pho-Bo-Ga 2** *(843 Somerset St. W., 234-7089, phoboga2.com)*, open daily until 5 a.m., the 24-hour **Zak's Diner** *(14 Byward Market, 241-2401, zaksdiner.com)*, or the 24-hour **Elgin Street Diner** *(374 Elgin St., 237-9700, elginstreetdiner.com)*.

LAUGH IT UP

For some of the best in live comedy, you can't really go wrong with the old standard, the Ottawa location of Mark Breslin's national chain of **Yuk Yuk's Comedy Clubs** *(88 Albert St., 236-5233, yukyuks.com)*; but don't overlook Little Italy, which has its own small club, **Absolute Comedy** *(412 Preston St., 233-8000, absolutecomedy.ca)*, with seven shows a week, running Wednesday to Sunday.

SOUNDS LIKE FUN

A fun thing to do late at night (wandering home from a pub, perhaps) is to walk through the sound sculpture called **V.I.P.** on the grounds of the new **Ottawa City Hall** *(110 Laurier Ave. W.)*, on the walkway from Laurier running between the two buildings. Designed like a kind of walk-in theremin, the piece is activated by motion, and plays a range of sound depending on where you stand and what you do between them (the city seems only to turn it off as winter approaches). Currently owned by the City of Ottawa, the piece was made by Michael Bussiere in 1994.

Photo: John W. MacDonald

the few remaining (as they claim) "historically rich, heritage buildings." Otherwise, there's **Helsinki Lounge** *(15 George St., 241-2868, Helsinki.ca)*, or the **Aloha Room** beneath Barrymore's *(323 Bank St., 233-0307, barrymores.on.ca)*, where you can get pints and hear the DJ spin tunes from your older brother's record collection. You might even see some musicians hanging out from shows upstairs, or maybe Gord Downie from the Tragically Hip, just passing through town. Still, I prefer the lounge's original name: Pete's Nervous Onion.

Gay Ottawa

Photo: Lois Siegel

Despite its sleepy government veneer, Ottawa is home to a vibrant gay, lesbian, bisexual, and transgender population. For proof, just look at the number of bars for the LGBTQ community. The oldest (still existing) hangout is the **Centretown Pub** *(340 Somerset St. W., 594-0233)*, with its heritage architecture and outdoor patio. Predominantly for men, there's **Swizzles Bar & Grill** *(246-B Queen St., 232-4200, swizzles.ca)*, with special nights that feature karaoke hosted by Swizzles regular Dog & Pony Sound, Sunday to Tuesday nights, as well as the **Dusty Owl Reading Series** *(dustyowl.com)* once or twice a month. **The Lookout Bar** *(41 York St., 789-1624, thelookoutbar.com)* not only has a great second-floor balcony overlooking the Byward Market, but has regular boys nights and girls nights. It also hosts karaoke with **Dog & Pony Sound** (see p. 133) on Wednesday nights (they sure do get around!).

For other gay clubs, there's the **Edge** *(212 Sparks St.)*, for the college crowd. Open at around 10 p.m., with events hosted by drag star Robin de Cradle, the place doesn't get rippin' until midnight. The rooftop patio, four floors above the basement bar, is open during the summer. For a more conservative feel, there's **Heaven** *(400A Dalhousie St., 482-9898, clubheaven. ca)*, a three-storey club with regular events. **Helsinki Lounge** *(15 George St., 241-2868, Helsinki.ca)* has drag shows and dancing on Wednesday nights, and, according to sources, the quickest pick-ups in the city. **Touché** *(87 Clarence St., 241-8787, touchelounge. ca)* is good for cheap drinks and cheap dates, complete with an illuminated dance floor. If adventure is your thing, checkout **Breathless** *(318 Lisgar St., breathlessottawa. com)*, a BDSM community space (above Venus Envy), for swingers and public sex types. **One In Ten** *(216 Bank St., 563-0110)* is a sex shop and adult video store, with a back room with glory holes, open 24 hours. There are bathhouses too, including **Club Ottawa Baths** *(1069 Wellington St., 722-8978)*, with a steam room, sauna, showers, and videos, or **Steamworks for Men** *(487 Lewis St., 230-8431)* with sauna, whirlpool, steam room, and "glory holes" (both venues open 24 hours). If you have to ask what glory holes are, then you probably shouldn't be going in there.

For further information, check out *gayottawa.com*.

Best Place for Blues

If you can't wait for July to get to **Bluesfest** *(ottawa-bluesfest.ca)*, check out the **Rainbow Bistro** *(76 Murray St., 241-5123, therainbow.ca)*, the original home of Ottawa's blues, jazz, and swing scene, offering a friendly, cozy atmosphere with live performances throughout the year. Jeff Healey, Powder Blues, Fathead, Mumbo Jumbo Voodoo Combo, and Roxanne Potvin have all graced the stage over the 20 years the club has been in existence, and they recently put out a

BARE ESSENTIALS

Maybe it's got something to do with this town being filled with normally buttoned-down businessmen and government types who need a — ahem — release valve now and again, but Ottawa has a lot to choose from in the way of strip clubs (or exotic dance bars, if you must). Some of Ottawa's old standards (that I still recommend) include **Barbarella's Diamond Cabaret** *(340 Queen St., 234-8709)*, **Barefax** *(27 York St., 562-1313)*, and **Fanny's Cabaret** *(128 York St., 241-0445)*. With 40 dancers daily, pool tables, catering, and full handicap accessibility, the **NuDen** *(1560 Triole St. and 1595 St Laurent Blvd., nuden. net)* even offers complimentary cover charge and coat check with any hotel room key from the Ottawa area.

TAKE A GAMBLE

If gambling is more your style, cross one of our inter-provincial bridges to get to **Casino Du Lac-Leamy** *(1 Boul. du Casino, 819-772-2100, casino-du-lac-leamy.com)* in Gatineau, whether for the casino itself, which includes 64 gambling tables and 1,870 slot machines, or for one of their many shows in **Le Théâtre du Casino** (recent performances include Cathy Gauthier, the Led Zeppelin Experience, Marie-Chantal Toupin, and André-Philippe Gagnon). How often do you get to spend an evening drinking in a lounge that has its own heliport?

They even have docking facilities for 20 boats and complete banking services, including a foreign exchange office. Come for the sound and light shows, stay for the gambling, but leave all your bankcards at home (to avoid temptation). Dress code in effect. Shuttle buses are available from downtown hotels.

retrospective CD of some of their favourite performers. A bit farther outside the downtown core is **Tucson's** *(2440 Bank St., 738-7596, tucsonblues.com)* where you'll find what they claim is "the best in food and blues."

Karaoke-Dokie

To unleash your inner Avril, there are a number of bars and other establishments in Ottawa that offer karaoke. One of the best is **Dog & Pony Sound** *(dogandponysound.com)* which takes its show to various establishments around town. Currently, you can find them at the **Royal Britannia Pub** *(Mon. and Thu. nights; 1475 Richmond Rd., 820-5050)*, the **Bytown Tavern** *(Wed. nights; 292 Elgin St., 231-3888)*, the **Cock & Lion** *(Thu. nights; 202 Sparks St., 233-0080)*, **Puzzles Sports Bar** *(Fri. nights; 344 Richmond Rd., 728-3024)*, and **O'Brien's Eatery and Pub** *(Fri. and Sat. nights; 1146 Heron Rd., 731-8752)*. As mentioned in "Gay Ottawa" (p. 131), they also do a show regularly at **Swizzles** *(Sun., Tue., and Fri. nights; 246 Queen St., 232-4200)*, **Go Go's Bar and Lounge** *(Sun. nights; 349 Dalhousie St., 860-1116)*, and the **LookOut** *(Wed. nights; 41 York St., 789-1624)*.

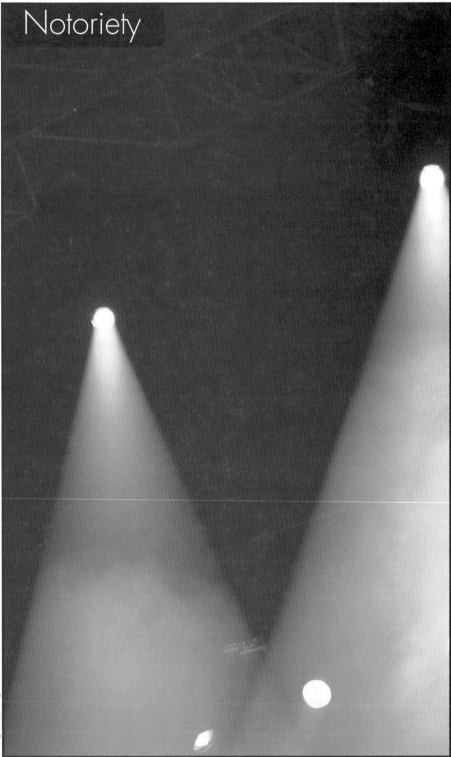

Notoriety

Despite whatever mild-mannered reputation Ottawa may have, the city's history is rife with roughneck tales of debauchery, riots, and malfeasance going back decades. Here are a few examples of tales seldom told that could easily change your mind about this city and its residents.

The Stony Monday Riots

In the early 19th century, the construction of the Rideau Canal brought large numbers of recently arrived Irish Catholic labourers into the area. After the canal was completed, and with increased unemployment in the region, the Irish Catholics became restless and revived old animosities with the French, English, and Protestant Irish. A group of disgruntled Irish known as the **Shiners** began to wage campaigns against French raftsmen and the Protestant fraternal order the Orangemen, escalating from street fights and bar brawls to a series of assaults and murders in 1837 (this period of Ottawa Valley history, 1837–1845, became known as the "Shiners' Wars"). The end of the Shiner terror came when their leader, **Peter Aylen**, left Ottawa for Aylmer after a series of particularly brutal attacks, but tensions among the various groups remained.

Most of the affluent Englishmen who lived in Uppertown (now Centretown) were Tories, while the French and Irish were Reformers. The Tories spent much of the 1840s incensed at the Reformist-minded politics of Lord Elgin, then Governor General of Canada. After riots started in Montreal, where Tories burnt down the Parliament Building located there, Elgin was prompted to look for another capital for Canada. When His Lordship announced plans to visit Bytown in September of 1849, the people of Lowertown began preparing a royal welcome. Uppertowners, meanwhile, argued that Elgin should be ignored, and a meeting was called in the Byward Market to discuss the situation. The gathering on September 17 erupted into another riot. Stones were thrown, mayhem broke out, and one person was shot on what became known as "Stony Monday." The British militia was called in to block the Lowertowners from advancing into Uppertown the following day, and the riot was dispersed.

Murdered MP

THE LATE HON. THOMAS D'ARCY McGEE.
From a Photograph by Notman. See page 136

One of Canada's early political assassinations occurred in Ottawa on Sparks Street. On April 7, 1868, poet, Member of Parliament, and Father of Confederation **Thomas D'Arcy McGee** (see photo) walked home after a particularly late session and was shot dead in the doorway of the rooming house where he was staying. A reward of $2,000 was offered to anyone who could bring the assassin to justice. Soon after, **Patrick James Whelan**, a tailor and Fenian sympathizer (Irish nationalists who brought their fight against England to the colonies) was convicted of the murder, though, years later, it was suggested that Whelan was chosen as a scapegoat. Held for months in the county jail (now the site of the Youth Hostel on Nicholas Street), Whelan was executed on the gallows outside the courthouse before a huge crowd on February 11, 1869. This was the last public execution in Canada. The Smith & Wesson Tip-up revolver that Whelan allegedly used in the crime was sold at auction to the Museum of Civilization in 2005 for over $100,000 (it had been held in a family collection for years, perhaps even going as far back as the event). As of 2000, the bullet was in the possession of the Ontario Archives, but when the 2005 sale of the gun brought attention to the story, the organization informed the Royal Canadian Mounted Police that it had gone missing sometime within the last five years.

A plaque has since been erected in front of the Royal Bank Building at 142 Sparks Street, identifying the location where McGee was assassinated. Just down the block, at the corner of Sparks and O'Connor Streets, printer George Desbarats (forebear of journalist Peter Desbarats and his daughter, poet Michelle Desbarats), who owned the rooming house where his friend McGee was staying, had originally put up the first memorial plaque soon after his McGee's death. After it was erected, Desbarats had received an anonymous warning that his printing establishment would be destroyed; and sure enough, it was lost to a fire in 1869, barely a year after McGee's assassination.

HEAVE HI, HEAVE HI HO

French-Canadian Ottawa Valley folk hero **Big Joe Mufferaw** (based on real-life 19th-century figure Joseph Montferrand) was lionized for his exploits as a mighty woodsman. He was also celebrated as a protector of French interests and opponent of the combative Irish Shiners. Big Joe was even immortalized in song ("Heave hi heave hi ho / The best man in Ottawa was Mufferaw Joe") by that inveterate Canadian mythmaker, folk singer Stompin' Tom Connors. Over the years, tales of Montferrand's physical feats in the Ottawa Valley, including an epic, bloody battle in which he fought 150 Shiners, turned him into a Paul Bunyanesque character. The building on Rue Laurier in Gatineau that currently houses the **Palais de Justice** is named for this local hero.

THE COLD WAR'S BIRTHPLACE?

The Cold War was inauspiciously launched at 511 Somerset Street West, in an apartment building now adjacent to the Beer Store. Don't believe it? On September 5, 1945, Russian-born **Igor Gouzenko**, posted to the Soviet Embassy in Ottawa as a cipher clerk, walked into the offices of the late daily the *Ottawa Journal* and, in essence, defected. He brought with him 109 carefully selected documents that he had been collecting for weeks, establishing conclusively the existence of a Soviet spy ring in North America. A royal commission was appointed the following February to investigate. In 2003, a plaque for Gouzenko (who, with his family, was given a new identity and relocated by the Canadian government) was erected in Dundonald Park across from his former home. Gouzenko, who had adopted an assumed name, died in 1982 in Mississauga.

Cold War, Hot Sex

It's often said that there haven't been many sex scandals on Parliament Hill simply because the exploits that have probably gone on haven't been revealed to the public. (One wonders about Prime Minister Pierre Trudeau's days and nights in office.) A scandal that did surface was the tale of **Gerda Munsinger**. An East German prostitute and Soviet spy, Munsinger got herself involved with a number of high-ranking Canadian government officials in the late 1950s, including cabinet ministers George Hees and Pierre Sévigny, much to the embarrassment of Prime Minister John Diefenbaker. While her affair with Hees was brief, she carried on a three-year relationship with Sévigny. Dubbed the **"Munsinger Affair,"** the scandal only became public in 1966 when Minister of Justice Lucien Cardin spoke out of turn during debate in Parliament. He not only got her name wrong, but revealed the scandal a good five years after she had been deported to East Germany, and three years after Sévigny had quietly resigned from Diefenbaker's cabinet. Despite the fact that the government claimed she had since died of leukemia, *Toronto Star* reporter Robert Reguly found her alive and well in Munich, West Germany, where she confirmed the story. Not only that, according to an interview Reguly did years later with *CTV.ca*, Munsinger revealed that he was inadequate in the sack, and told him, "As a lover, you make a great politician." Dubbed a security risk and "ruined by the Munsinger affair," Sévigny was eventually cleared of charges of disloyalty, but he spent the rest of his life in isolation. The scandal was the basis of the 1992 feature film *Gerda*.

The Parliamentary Bathroom Bomber

On the afternoon of May 18, 1966, after moving from failed jobs to failed businesses and blaming everyone but himself, Toronto resident **Paul Chartier** focused his unhappiness on the Canadian government, and planned to throw an explosive in the House of Commons during question period. Working his way through the Parliament Buildings, Chartier discovered that the Public Gallery was full, forcing him to move to the (then) Ladies' Gallery on the third floor. Here he entered a washroom to light the explosive, and planned to return quickly to toss it to the floor of the House. Misjudging the length of the fuse, he managed only to blow up himself and the washroom; he was killed instantly. For the first time in history, the sittings of the House were temporarily suspended, resuming an hour after the incident.

Diplomatic Non-Immunity

In 2001, Russian diplomat **Andrei Knyazev**, working as first secretary at the embassy, was driving home from an ice-fishing party, where he had allegedly consumed considerable amounts of alcohol, when his car skidded onto the sidewalk after missing a turn in the quiet residential neighbourhood of New Edinburgh. He struck and killed 50-year-old Catherine MacLean, a prominent labour lawyer, and seriously injured Catherine Dore, whose dog was also killed. Knyazev refused a breathalyzer test, and invoked his diplomatic immunity, enraging Canadians across the country. The Russian ambassador immediately ordered Knyazev back to Moscow. A year later, he was sentenced by the Russians to four years in a "village colony," where he would sleep in medium-security barracks, report to guards twice a day, and spend his time labouring either in farming or forestry. Originally, the embassy had denied that anyone there had reported any sort of accident, and when questioned, Knyazev denied even having a drink that day. Both Deputy Prime Minister John Manley and Foreign Affairs Minister Bill Graham were adamant that zero tolerance of drunk driving be upheld, however, and apparently the Russian government agreed – they introduced their own zero tolerance policy for their diplomats abroad.

Embassy Under Seige

On March 12, 1985, a squad of terrorists armed with assault rifles and hand grenades stormed the Turkish embassy. It all started early that morning, when a rented U-Haul van backed up to the wall of the embassy and three heavily armed members of the Armenian Revolutionary Army leaped out, scaled the wall, shot and killed a guard, and worked their way into the building's inner sanctum. They demanded the return of

I KNOW MY (HIC) RIGHTS

When **Margaret Trudeau Kemper**, ex-wife of former Prime Minister Pierre Trudeau, was charged with drunk driving in 2004, she got off on a technicality based on a violation of the Charter of Rights. Originally claiming he had pulled her over for a speeding violation, the arresting officer ultimately admitted that his speedometer wasn't calibrated, so the defense was able to argue that his stopping her was unwarranted. It also didn't help that while at the police station she had been kept in a locked room, unable to call out, and the policeman didn't properly telephone her lawyers, upon her request.

their land and the acknowledgment of the genocide that was carried out on the Armenians by the Turks in 1915. During the siege, the Turkish ambassador, Coşkun Kirca, was forced to throw himself out of a second-storey window. Arriving on the scene, Ottawa police constable Michel Prud'Homme kept the ambassador, who was severely injured by the fall, hidden from the terrorists for hours, earning Prud'Homme the Medal of Bravery. Once captured, the three gunmen were sentenced to 25 years in prison without parole.

Before the attack of 1985, many foreign diplomats had complained about the lax security for embassies in Canada. The 1985 incident caused Prime Minister Brian Mulroney's government to act quickly, leading to the creation of Canada's top-secret commando unit, **Joint Task Force Two.**

Some Rapid Robbers

The **Stopwatch Gang**, led by Ottawa's own **Paddy Mitchell** (who grew up in Little Italy), **Stephen Reid** (of Massey, Ontario), and **Lionel Wright**, are perhaps Canada's most infamous bank robbers. The trio, whose orchestrated meticulous heists never took longer than 90 seconds, robbed more than 100 banks and armoured cars during the 1970s and 80s in the United States and Canada. Their most notorious job was a 1974 gold heist (worth $750,000) at the Ottawa airport, earning themselves a place on the FBI's most-wanted list. The gang's exploits were detailed in several movies, including *Point Break* (1991) and *The Heist* (2001), as well as in the book *The Stopwatch Gang* (1992) by *Toronto Sun* reporter Greg Weston, and in Mitchell's own memoir, *This Bank Robber's Life*, which he wrote in prison and sold over the Internet. While still in jail, Reid wrote his own book, a semi-autobiographical novel titled *Jackrabbit Parole*. Through this book he met his editor, West Coast poet and writer Susan Musgrave, and in 1986 they married while he was still imprisoned. Upon his release a year later, he and Musgrave attempted to live a quiet life on Vancouver Island, and had a child as well. He appeared as a rifle-toting security guard in a 15-second cameo (as well as acting as the film's bank heist consultant) in the independent movie *Four Days* (1999). Unfortunately, in the spring of 1999 in Victoria, BC, his heroin addiction resulted in a return to crime and a botched robbery and shootout; currently, Reid (see

HOSTELLING HOOSEGOW

Interested in knowing what it's like to sleep in a prison cell? Well, you can at the **Hostelling International Ottawa Jail Youth Hostel**. And when you want to leave, you don't have to attend a parole hearing. Located in the centre of downtown, this facility served as the **Carleton County Gaol** from 1862–1972, and now offers accommodation in converted jail cells, with private as well as shared rooms (ideal for families and groups). Here, you might even get to stay in the cell that once held Patrick James Whelan, convicted of assassinating Thomas D'Arcy McGee (see p 136). *75 Nicholas St., 235-2595, 1-866-299-1478, hihostels.com*

photo above) remains in prison. The leader of the gang, Patrick "Paddy" Mitchell, called "North America's most famous, most successful and, especially, most likeable bank robber of our time" by his son, grew up on Preston Street in Ottawa, and died of cancer on in 2007 in a US prison while serving a 65-year sentence. Wright served his sentence, and according to a 2005 report from the CBC, worked as an accountant for Corrections Canada. The gold from the airport robbery in 1974 was never recovered.

Gold Fish

Ottawa, as the site of the **Bank of Canada**, played a central role in **Operation Fish**, an undertaking initiated in 1940 to provide safekeeping for the assets of Britain, Norway, France, and Belgium in Canada for the duration of World War II. Six ships carried combined gold and securities from the four allied countries via Britain; secretly unloaded in Halifax, the reserves were transported to Montreal by train, then to Ottawa, where the 60 million ounces of gold were loaded onto trucks at night and ferried to the basement of the Bank of Canada on Wellington Street under the watchful eye of armed guards disguised in simple overalls. The crates were unloaded and stacked by two 30-member teams who, although they worked 24 hours a day, were unable to keep up with the number of crates delivered. The backlog of 1,500 unopened crates of gold that lined the halls of the basement soon required a contingent of RCMP officers to guard it round the clock. But it's hard to keep any secret for long. One can only presume that once the war ended, the gold was just as secretly slipped back out of the country and returned to its owners.

THE FEDERAL STASH

In the 1970s, Health and Welfare Canada asked the Central Experimental Farm in Ottawa to grow several types of **marijuana** for medical research. A crop was quietly planted and kept in the middle of a well-fenced cornfield (before you get your hopes up, the crop has long since been replaced). Eventually, when the plants grew taller than the surrounding corn, a higher fence with barbed wire was installed to guard against theft. Eventually a guard tower and watchdogs were introduced to deter organized and/or disorganized potheads from getting even that far. Otherwise, to get bongs and seeds in Ottawa, check out the counterculture variety store **Crosstown Traffic** (593-C Bank St., 234-1210; 396 Athlone Ave., 728-4800; crosstowntraffic.ca).

DEATH OF A FLYING ACE

On March 12, 1930, **Lieutenant-Colonel William George "Billy" Barker** was killed in a crash at Rockcliffe airport in Ottawa while demonstrating a new training plane. Since Barker was a highly skilled pilot and there was no indication of mechanical malfunction, it has been theorized that Barker deliberately crashed the plane, thus committing suicide. During World War I, he had brought down 53 German planes and was praised as a hero, but once home after the war, his years were filled with constant pain and depression. One of his early planes was the Sopwith two-seater Dove, which was later reconstructed and transferred to Canada for permanent display at the **Canadian War Museum** (see p 36).

Rest in Peace

The Ottawa region is relatively safe for residents and visitors alike. Nevertheless, the area has been the site of a few strange and disturbing fatalities over the years. Hopefully these are the exceptions that prove the rule:

- In the town of Perth, just an hour's drive west of the city, **the last fatal duel in Ontario** occurred on June 13, 1833. Two law students and former friends, John Wilson and Robert Lyon, had been quarrelling over remarks Lyon made concerning a local teacher, Elizabeth Hughes, whom both men were interested in. The outcome: Lyon was killed, and Wilson was charged with murder. Wilson, who was eventually acquitted, married Elizabeth Hughes and later became an MP and a judge.

- In 1882, a man **committed suicide in the Notre-Dame Cathedral Basilica** (otherwise known as La Basilique Cathédral de Notre-Dame, 385 Sussex Dr.), putting a bullet in his head after a mass. A gang of priests had to be sent in to re-consecrate the church afterwards.

- In 1998, 21-year-old Ottawa resident Jérôme Charron died in an accident on a **"reverse bungee"** (also known as a "catapult bungee" or "ejector seat") a ride at the **SuperEx** at Lansdowne Park on Bank Street. The ride, called "The Rocket Launcher," consists of two poles feeding two elastic ropes down to a two-passenger car; once released from its electro-magnetic latch, the car is shot straight upwards with an acceleration of 4.8 Gs, with a maximum altitude of 55 metres (180 feet). Instead, the ride hurled him 40 metres (130 feet) into the air before his harness became detached, causing him to plummet to his death. In 2000, the American firm responsible for the ride was fined $145,000 for the incident. Provincial inspectors had apparently inspected and approved the ride just four days before the accident, but did not inspect the faulty strap.

- University of Waterloo PhD student **Ardeth Wood** was 27 years old when she went missing while cycling along the Aviation Parkway on August 6, 2003. After an extensive search by police and community volunteers (the largest search operation ever undertaken by the Ottawa Police Service), her body was found on August 11 by a specially trained OPP cadaver dog, just metres from where her abandoned bicycle had been found. Her murder launched one of the largest manhunts in Canadian history. It also opened up a dark chapter in Ottawa's own history, as women all over the city suddenly no longer felt safe to leave their homes after dark, especially along remote bike paths. In October 2005, Chris Myers, a 25-year-old Ottawa resident, was found in North Bay, Ontario and charged with the murder, as well as four other counts of sexual assaults.

- In the winter of 2006, the naked body of a seven-month-pregnant Vanier woman, **Kelly Morrisseau**, was found in Gatineau Park, having been stabbed more than a dozen times. With accusations by members of her family in June 2007 that the attention on her murder had waned because she was Aboriginal, the Assembly of First Nations put up a substantial reward for information, adding $2,000 to the $2,000 already offered by Crimestoppers.

From Outbreak to Opening

In June 1847, a **typhus** epidemic broke out in Ottawa's Lowertown very soon after the Sisters of Charity constructed the building that would eventually become Ottawa's first **General Hospital** (being little more than a wooden house on St. Patrick Street at the time). The disease was thought to have been brought over with the thousands of Irish immigrants fleeing the Potato Famine. By the following May, 167 of the 619 people afflicted had died. The overflow of patients was quarantined on the west side of the Rideau Canal in wooden sheds, under boats, and in tents. Unfortunately, with all the fear of infection from typhus and smallpox, the last thing any of the residents of Sandy Hill wanted in their neighbourhood was a hospital of any kind, and as late as 1879, a couple of them were even burned down by locals. After the typhus epidemic had subsided, the Sisters purchased six lots at what is now Sussex Drive and Bruyère Street (previously Water Street) to build a new General Hospital, which was finally opened to patients in 1866.

BUTT OUT

Heather Crowe. Name doesn't ring a bell? You might have seen her in all those Canadian anti-smoking public service announcements a few years ago, whether on television or in movie theatres. Crowe, who was a waitress for 40 years, was dying of lung cancer, despite having never smoked a day in her life. She contracted the disease through second-hand smoke she inhaled at work. After her diagnosis, she spent her last four years leading a nation-wide battle against second-hand smoke and influenced policy through her anti-smoking activism across Canada. Sadly, she died in 2006 at age 61. Her last 14 years were spent working at Moe's infamous Newport Restaurant

in Westboro; a year after she died, Health Promotion Minister Jim Watson presented owner Moe Atallah with the Heather Crowe Award for making his workplace smoke-free and voluntarily stopping the sale of cigarettes in the Newport convenience store. Crowe is the subject of a short documentary film, *Heather Crowe's Legacy: An Ordinary Canadian's Extraordinary Gift*, which is available free to schools, community and church groups, book clubs, and to those in the workplace by calling Cynthia Callard at **Physicians for a Smoke-Free Canada** at 233-4878.

A Pox on Thee!

The smallpox isolation facility on **Porter's Island**, on the Rideau River between Old St. Patrick Street on one side and New Edinburgh Park on the other, was typical of the types of quarantine arrangements during epidemics, with small shanty-like shacks housing patients who, for the most part, quickly died where they lay. The facility operated until the early part of the 1900s and treated victims of typhoid and influenza as well as smallpox. Between January and March 1911, there were 987 cases of typhoid reported in Ottawa, 83 of which resulted in death. In 1910, a consultant recommended regular chlorination to treat the water, and the Gatineau Hills as an alternate source, because an earlier typhoid outbreak was traced to the use of an emergency intake valve in Nepean Bay (located on the Ottawa River below the Royal Canadian Mint at the base of the Nepean River behind Parliament Square). The island now exists as a park and is a great site for birding, with urban fishing available, and a section of private property. It is also home to the Island Lodge retirement centre. A footbridge provides access from St. Patrick Street (except during the winter months, when it remains closed).

Kaboom!

Just before noon on May 29, 1929, Ottawa residents were startled by a **violent gas explosion** in the main sewer line between the Ottawa River and Centretown. Over the next nine hours, a series of explosions ran the stretch of the main line more than five kilometres (3 mi) long, shooting manhole covers three storeys into the air in an area stretching from Sandy Hill (roughly the intersection of Cartier and Waverley Streets) through New Edinburgh and into the suburb of Eastview. Surprisingly, only one person was killed (a janitor in the basement of the building at the centre of the explosion), but a number of buildings were destroyed, including St. Martin's Reform Episcopal Church in New Edinburgh. After the dust had settled, officials made inquiries into the cause, but the findings were inconclusive, despite the fact that residents along the line had reported the smell of gas to the city for months prior to the explosion. One outcome, though, was a bylaw passed to stop volatile liquids from being dumped into sewers.

Great Balls of Fire

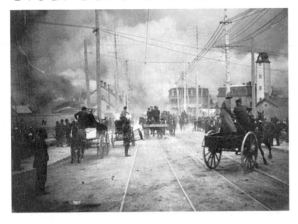

Though a blaze that raged through town in 1900 is generally referred to as the **"Great Ottawa Fire,"** the city has been plagued by a multitude of infernos throughout its history. (And what else would a great lumber town fear in the 1800s but the fiery ravages?) Settled long before Ottawa, the city of Hull (now called Gatineau) would have been much larger now, it is often said, if it weren't for the fires that kept taking most of the city during the 1870s and 80s. As for Ottawa, it didn't help that, until 1874, the town relied on volunteer firefighters, many of whom would simply ignore the fire bell when it rang, and when the city started offering a cash reward to water carriers that reached fires first, competing companies broke into brawls when they should have been dousing flames.

On April 26, 1900, the Great Ottawa Fire started on the Hull side, causing devastation throughout much of the city, and crossed into Ottawa via the bridge at Booth Street. The Ottawa fire department turned out en masse to fight the blaze, and calls were put out to Montreal, Smiths Falls, Brockville, Peterborough, and Toronto for additional help, as the blaze sent up plumes of smoke that could be seen for hundreds of kilometres. Damage extended as far south as **Dow's Lake**, and lumber baron **J. R. Booth** lost 55 million board feet of lumber. Fortunately, the high limestone cliffs separating the Chaudière district from the rest of Ottawa, coupled with a drop in wind speed, prevented the flames from overtaking the Parliament Buildings. Still, the affected area encompassed a one-kilometre (0.5-mi) wide strip from the Chaudière Falls south for four kilometres (2.5 mi)

THINGS THAT GO BUMP IN THE NIGHT

If you like to get your spook on, take part in one of the capital's **Haunted Walks**, a series of spine-chilling walking tours around the downtown, and get a glimpse of the darker, haunted history of the nation's capital. Walks take place during the day, or in the evening by lantern-light, with tours in English and French, including "Crime and Punishment Jail Tour," "The Naughty Ottawa Pub Walk," "The Original Haunted Walk of Ottawa," and "Ghosts and the Gallows." Will you see the ghost of Prime Minister Mackenzie King? Or will you run into the spirit of Thomas D'Arcy McGee? You will only find out once you secure your reservation. *232-0344, hauntedwalk.com*

to Carling Avenue, leaving seven dead, 3,000 buildings destroyed, and 15,000 people homeless. The area known as **LeBreton Flats**, just west of the downtown core by Scott and Booth Streets, has been almost completely vacant since, with new development beginning only over the past few years, with the construction of the new **Canadian War Museum**.

Bridge to Disaster

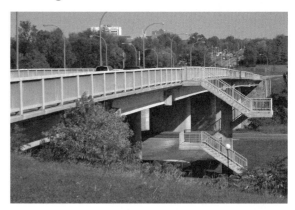

Nine workers were killed and 57 others were injured in Ottawa's worst construction disaster when the south span of the **Heron Road Bridge** collapsed without warning into the Rideau River on August 10, 1966. Most of the workers killed were crushed beneath thousands of tons of wet concrete. Through all the dust and confusion, it was not until early the next day before everyone had been accounted for. An army of rescuers (including the mayor of Ottawa, Don Reid) worked their way through the rubble to free the trapped and injured workers. All available cars, trucks, and even a military helicopter were pressed into service to take the injured to hospital. It was almost another two years before the bridge was rebuilt and opened to traffic. In 1987, a plaque listing the dead was erected in a boulder just west of the bridge along Heron Road by the Building Trades Union.

A Walk on the Wilde Side

In May 1882, the infamous playwright **Oscar Wilde** made a two-day stopover in Ottawa during a lecture tour of North America, with his performance making the front page of the *Ottawa Citizen*. During his stay, he visited a sitting of Parliament, and met **Frances Richards**, a young Ottawa portrait painter. The following year Richards visited Wilde in Paris and eventually moved to London in 1887. In late December that same year, she painted his portrait which, according to Christopher Millard, a contemporary London art critic, was the inspiration for Wilde's novel, *The Picture of Dorian Gray*. Richards, who later became Mrs W. E. Rowley, Esq., had ties to another Canadian expatriate living in London, Mrs Augusta Ross, daughter of Robert Baldwin, the premier of the Province of Canada (1848–51). And, according to many of Wilde's biographers, it was Ross's third son, Robbie, who, through a meeting with Wilde, helped the famous writer recognize his homosexuality (he had previously shown little interest in the male sex and was even known as quite the ladies' man). "Faithful Robbie" became not only Wilde's first recorded male lover, but was with Wilde when he died, in Paris in 1900, disgraced and abandoned by the public.

Rich & Famous, Ottawa-Style

Ottawa socialite **Marlen Cowpland** is famous in the city for a number of things, including being the second and current wife of former Corel CEO **Michael Cowpland**, as well as for her daring fashions and her short-lived local Ottawa cable channel fashion show, *Celebrity Pets*. Some of her more outlandish exploits include: sporting spectacular over-the-top outfits at various Ottawa-area events, dyeing her pet poodle various colours (depending on the occasion), and being pulled over for speeding (and allegedly let off because she was on her way to a charity function). Some of the guests on her cable show included classical guitarist **Liona Boyd** (with cat), psychic **JoJo Savard** (with Maltese), Hollywood producer/director **Garry Marshall** (with two cocker spaniels), singer **Jann Arden** (with three cats), and professional wrestler **Bret "The Hitman" Hart** (with pug).

Michael Cowpland, along with Terry Matthews, founded **Mitel Networks** in Ottawa in 1973. The company developed and sold PBX (communications) systems, which made both Cowpland and Matthews multi-millionaires. Matthews went on to establish Newbridge Networks while Cowpland founded

THE GIRL NEXT DOOR

It's good to know that the Ottawa Valley's wholesome image is being represented abroad by **Shannon Tweed** – yes, *that* Shannon Tweed. A prolific actress and, perhaps more famously, Playboy Playmate of the Year 1982, the St. John's, Newfoundland-born Tweed represented the Ottawa Valley in the 1978 Miss Canada Pageant, placing fourth. Around the same time, her rich boyfriend opened a restaurant in Ottawa in her honour called Shannon's, but neither the restaurant nor their relationship lasted. You can currently catch her on the reality TV show *Gene Simmons Family Jewels*, with her partner, KISS front man Gene Simmons, and their two teenaged children.

GIVE PEACE A CHANCE

Most people know about **John Lennon and Yoko Ono's** famous "bed-in" at a Montreal hotel in 1969. But let's not forget: they also proclaimed, "Plug peace, it's merchandise!" to a large crowd of students at the University of Ottawa's Simard Hall during that same Canadian tour. They actually made two Ottawa stops, first at the University of Ottawa, then to meet with Prime Minister Pierre Trudeau on Parliament Hill, and Health Minister John Munro. The university visit was organized by Students' Association President (and future federal finance minister) Allan Rock and Hugh Segal (who later worked for Prime Minister Brian Mulroney). While at the university, John and Yoko gave a "Seminar on World Peace." For further information on their trip, check out the Ottawa Beatles Website *(beatles.ncf.ca)*, where you'll find a whole slew of information and photos (including George Harrison's stay at the Chateau Laurier in February of the same year).

Cowpland Research Laboratory, which was later shortened to **Corel**. After successfully fending off an insider trading probe, he left the company in 2000, and currently heads **ZIM Techologies**, a wireless technology firm. If you get a chance, drive by the Cowplands' 20,000-square-foot home on Soper Place, assessed for tax purposes at more than $10 million. There's nothing in Ottawa that can compare to a house of mirrored glass and copper-coloured accents in one of the ritziest sections of Rockcliffe Park.

The Cat Man of Parliament Hill

Photo: Klaus J. Gerken

Of all of the official positions held in this government town, perhaps the least known, yet no less essential, is that of "Cat Man." Tucked in a small compound behind the wrought-iron fence west of the Centre Block, a population of feral cats has lived behind the Hill since the late 1970s, currently fed by presiding cat man **René Chartrand**. He took over from the original Cat Lady, the late **Irene Desormeaux**, in 1987, and has since gone to the Hill twice a day, every day, to dole out kibble (costing some $6,000 a year) purchased using money donated through discreet donation boxes affixed to the railings, as well as from his own pockets. Completely outside of the official designation of the Hill, the guides tend to skip the small shelters that house the feline brood, which have since been made more permanent, in wooden structures in the shape of the Parliament Buildings.

Call it what you will, *eight months of winter* or *four months of bad skiing*, living in Ottawa can often feel *plenty* hard during the winter months, and even through the balmiest of sunny, summer days. Here are some ways to keep yourself entertained, lavishly styled, or even just well-groomed, whatever time of the year.

City on the Grow

According to the 2006 Census, Ottawa is the fastest-growing G8 city with a population of 1,130,761 in the Ottawa-Gatineau area, putting us fourth behind Toronto, Montreal, and Vancouver (with Calgary and Edmonton very close behind). In 2001, city officials predicted a growth rate of 11.5 percent, but by 2006, had seen only a five percent growth in that time. For further details, see *statscan.ca*.

Where We Rank

In a 2007 survey, *MoneySense* magazine ranked Ottawa-Gatineau first out of 122 communities in Canada as economically the best place to live. At the same time, Ottawa was ranked 18th in the world among cities with the best quality of life by a global survey published by Mercer Human Resource Consulting, placing it third in Canada, after Vancouver and Toronto.

Queer Ottawa

Photo: Eric Vaillancourt

The first march for **gay and lesbian rights** on Parliament Hill on August 28, 1971 was far less violent than the infamous 1969 Stonewall riots in the US, but no less important. It marked the dawn of the modern gay and lesbian movement in Canada, and very specifically, in Ottawa. That day, about 100 gay men and lesbians walked through the rain to announce their demands to Parliament. Key players included the **Gay Day Committee of Toronto Gay Action**, who, a week before the march, presented the federal government with a brief called "We Demand," which included calls to create uniform heterosexual and homosexual age of consent and allow gays to serve in the military.

In Gary Kinsmen's book *The Regulation of Desire*, he talks about how the federal government worked very hard to regulate homosexuality through a series of national security campaigns conducted by the RCMP during the 1950s and 60s. According to Kinsmen, RCMP agents would set up camp in the basement tavern of the **Lord Elgin Hotel**, one of Ottawa's oldest gay hangouts, and take photographs of gay men through holes cut in newspapers. Despite this, a large network of closeted men and women existed in the capital, congregating at private dinner parties and weekend cottage gatherings.

Ottawa's first gay organization was formed in 1971, when seven men met at the home of Maurice Bélanger and Michael Black, calling themselves **Gays of Ottawa**. The group rented office space on the sixth floor of Pestalozzi College, a free-thinking institution located in an apartment building at Rideau and Chapel Streets (see p. 32).

During the 1970s, gay men in Ottawa were so besieged, their experience was referred to as the "Ottawa witch hunt," but while police surveillance, harassment, and arrest of gays in local parks increased, many charges (of gross indecency) were thrown out of the courts. A number of those arrested – many who had not yet come out to friends, family, or co-workers – had the added devastation of having their names published by the media. This led one man, Warren Zufelt, to commit suicide in 1979 on the day his name was mentioned in local newspapers as one of 18 men arrested in an Ottawa "sex scandal." NDP MLA for Ottawa Centre Michael Cassidy, reacting to Zufelt's death, wrote to the Minister of Justice and the Minister of Labour to protest police persecution of gays and called for the inclusion of "sexual orientation" in the Ontario Human Rights Code; after years of debate, protests, and campaigns, it was finally included on December 2, 1986.

CANADA'S FIRST GAY MAYOR?

According to Bruce Ricketts' Mysteries of Canada website (mysteriesofcanada.com), **Charlotte Whitton**, mayor of Ottawa in the 1950s and early 1960s, and the first female mayor of a Canadian city, had "lived for 32 years with her companion, Margaret Grier, whom she had met at Queen's University." Was Whitton our first gay mayor, in the days before such things were discussed? Perhaps it never turned into an issue, because Margaret Grier died in 1947 at the age of 55 years, well before Whitton got into office. According to Ricketts, Whitton is also known for this infamous quote: "Whatever women do they must do twice as well as men to be thought half as good. Luckily, this is not difficult."

Go For a Dip

Champagne Bath and the Plant Bath – now known respectively as the **Champagne Fitness Centre** and **Plant Recreation Centre** – were both built in 1924 to improve the hygiene and well being of the city's lower classes in the years before running water and bathing facilities were available in most homes. The Champagne Bath structure, which was originally home to a library, was designed by noted local architect **Werner Ernst Noffke** and named after Ottawa mayor Napoléon Champagne (1908, 1924). It became the city's first municipal pool and one of the first indoor pools in Ottawa. It was unusual for its salt water, which meant it did not need to be chlorinated. Until 1967, the facility was segregated with separate ground-level entrances for men and women. For a while, there was talk of closing the pool after the newer Le Patro was completed in the 1980s, but after public protest, the Champagne Bath was instead renovated and reopened in 1990. The Plant Bath, named after Frank H. Plant, then mayor of Ottawa (1921–23, 1930), was closed in 1997 after a long period of disrepair, only three years after being designated a heritage property. The building underwent extensive renovations and expansions, and was reopened in 2004. It now holds a semi-Olympic-sized pool as well as a leisure pool and a fitness centre. It also offers swimming lessons, fitness programs, and a variety of indoor and outdoor recreation programs.

Champagne Fitness Centre: 321 King Edward Ave., 224-4402
Plant Recreation Centre, 930 Somerset St. W. at Preston St., 232-3000

NOT THE WORLD'S COLDEST

Despite Canada's meteorological reputation, Ottawa is not the world's coldest capital. Though it did reach -38.9°C (-38.0°F) on December 29, 1933, this is only the second coldest temperature recorded in a world capital, after Ulaanbaatar, Mongolia, which has an average annual temperature of -1.3°C (29.6°F). Otherwise, Ottawa's annual average of 5.5°C (41.9°F) ranks it the seventh coldest world capital city, but third by mean January temperature, after Ulaanbaatar and Astana, Kazakhstan. This is why I spend most of January and February indoors.

Ingenious Ottawa

Inspired by the CBC-TV program *The Greatest Canadian Inventions*, we thought we'd present a list of a few of the great concepts devised by some of Ottawa's citizenry.

Green Genius

University of Ottawa professor and chemist **Dr Abdelhamid Sayari** and his research team spent three years developing a material that can absorb carbon dioxide contained in various industrial gases and prevent it from being released into the atmosphere, thus reducing the greenhouse gas emissions that cause global climate change.

R-r-r-roll up the R-r-r-rim

After three years of developing a different invention, Ottawa inventor **Paul Kind** introduced his "Rimroller," created to cleanly slice and unroll a Tim Hortons coffee cup rim in one motion, thus giving coffee drinkers easy access to the coffee chain's promotional give-a-ways (the notifications are hidden under the cup rim, which can be difficult to unroll). Considering that Tim Hortons sells in the area of 300 million take-out cups of coffee a year, the invention is not nearly as foolish as it may seem. With the help of L-D Tool & Die in nearby Stittsville, the Rimroller became a reality in 2006 and is available at Lee Valley Tools, and at $1.95, is just a bit more than the price of a cup of coffee. This is not the only creation from the fertile mind of Mr Kind. He also invented the Handyfold, to perfectly fold letters to fit into envelopes, and the Bookhug, to hold your book open for you while you read.

Photo: courtesy of Paul Kind

Founded in 2004 by two guys from Vancouver and Seattle respectively, the **World Naked Bike Ride** (*worldnakedbikeride.org*) is an international event with participants from numerous activist groups — including the Work Less Party of British Columbia, THONG (Topless Humans Organized for Natural Genetics) of Chicago, and Seattle's Naked Freedom Film Festival. WNBR's mandate is summed up best on their website: "We face automobile traffic with our naked bodies as the best way of defending our dignity and exposing the unique dangers faced by cyclists and pedestrians as well as the negative consequences we all face due to dependence on oil and other forms of non-renewable energy." Ottawa's annual version of this event began in June of 2005 with about nine participants (there were over 50 participants at the 2007 event). Here, the *au naturel* cyclists' route leads them from the fountain in Confederation Park (where there's body painting), then along Somerset Street West. Sometimes they'll even stop for gelato and a swim in the Ottawa River along the way. If you participate, be aware that traffic laws must be obeyed — otherwise, the only required accoutrement is a helmet.

Keeping Up the Pace

Dr John Alexander Hopps – originally from Winnipeg but a resident of Ottawa for many years – is known internationally as the inventor of the world's first heart pacemaker, introduced in 1951. In collaboration with Dr Wilfred Bigelow and Dr John Callaghan as part of the National Research Council of Canada (NRC), he spent most of his career at the Montreal Road branch of the NRC. Their creation was first implanted in a human body in 1958. Poignantly, the very device Dr Hopps had developed was implanted in his own chest 30 years after its invention to correct his erratic heartbeat.

A Close Shave

Photo: John W. MacDonald

If you're a devotee of traditional barbershops with the swirling barber poles and the old men swapping stories, check out either of the two locations of the **Imperial Barber Shop** (46½ Sparks St.; 275 Slater St., imperialbarbershop.com), or some of Ottawa's other options, including **Victoria Barber Shop** (9 O'Connor St., 284-5465), the **Glebe Barber Shop** (201–738 Bank St., 231-3343), or **Moderno Barber Shop** (116 Preston St., 236-5677). Looking for a different kind of barbershop? You can always check out a performance of Ottawa's own 85-plus chorus of the **Capital City Chorus** (capitalcitychorus.org), which will represent Ontario in the 2008 International Convention of the Barbershop Harmony Society in Nashville.

GET NUDE, DUDE!

If the World Naked Bike ride isn't enough for you, unfortunately there really aren't that many other places to get publicly naked in and around Ottawa (big surprise). Some options include: the relative privacy of the nude beach at beautiful **Meech Lake** in Gatineau Park, or the sketchier digs (not nearly as upscale as the first) nearby at the **Old Mill Falls**. Maps and other information can be found by checking out the Federation of Canadian Naturists website (fcn.ca), or the Ottawa Naturists (onno.ca).

Wishy-Washy

For a city that's had more than its share of dirty laundry, here are numerous opportunities to come clean: **Laundry Life** *(779 Bank St., 237-1483)* and **Centretown Laundry Co-op** *(153 Chapel St., 244-4524)* are both good self-serves, while **Tang Coin Laundry** *(609 Somerset St. W. 231-7468)* and **Market Laundry Room** *(286½ Dalhousie St., 241-6222)* both offer drop-off services. **Rideau Coinwash** *(436 Rideau St., 789-4400)* includes drop-off services as well as mending.

If you're a hockey history buff, go to **Majestic Cleaners & Laundry** *(551 Gladstone Ave. at Percy St., 236-1356)*, where you can kill time waiting for your whites to dry by reading the plaque outside that tells about the ice rink that used to occupy the building's lot. Some of the first **Stanley Cup playoff games** were played here (see p. 51), nearly a century ago.

Merry Christmas, Ottawa

With some 300,000 multi-coloured lights at roughly 70 sites along Confederation Boulevard, including Parliament Hill, the **National Capital Commission's Christmas Lights Across Canada** program runs from early December to early January every year.

Sure, the official lights on Parliament Hill are impressive, but there are also a number of other public buildings and private residences around Ottawa that present their own spectacular shows, which are well worth checking out. Some favourites include the trees outside the **Museum of Nature** (Metcalfe at McLeod Streets), the lights at **Confederation Park** on Elgin Street, 181 Clare Street (near Carling and Kirkwood Avenues), the housing development at the corner of Deschamps Street and the Vanier Parkway (one block north of Montreal Road), and the house at 2740 Kingwood Lane in Blossom Park, Gloucester, which is but one of many homes lit up on that stretch of street. At the house on 2455 Alta Vista Drive (one block north of Heron Road) you can let your kids have fun counting how many Santas there are in the display.

GET PSYCHIC-ED

You'd think a really *good* psychic wouldn't need to be called; she should just know to call you. In case that doesn't happen, make an appointment with palm and tarot card reader **Psychic Diana** (who describes herself as a "European gifted fortune teller and spiritual healer") to find out about the rest of your life. *235-9697 or 521-2424, psychicdiana.yp.ca*

LOW SELF-ESTEEM

Clearly, Ottawa needs to come to terms with its self-image. When UK poet **Jem Rolls** performs, he likes to poll his audiences on their "favourite" and "least favourite" cities. At the 2004 Fringe Festival in Ottawa, the audience's least favourite city was — Ottawa. According to Rolls, it was the first time an audience considered its hometown the worst.

PURE AT LAST

Located in an unassuming grey building in LeBreton Flats under Old Wellington Street is the **Fleet Street Pumping Station**. Opened in 1875 as Ottawa's first pumping station, it directs unfiltered water from the Ottawa River into the city's supply system. At first, it used the energy of Chaudière Falls to force untreated water into the system, until 1915 when an electric motor-driven station was built on Lemieux Island; a complete water purification plant was constructed in 1932. The station was built on the heels of a number of health epidemics in the Ottawa area, significantly reducing the amount of illness once city residents finally had access to clean drinking water.

Photo: Everdina Carter

If you can't wait for Christmas, check out the house at **158 Marier Avenue in Vanier**, featuring Santa and his reindeer in a glass-enclosed nativity scene, and a working fish tank in the front during the summer months. Just west of downtown, another decorated house is at **9 Grant Street** (just behind the Royal Bank on Wellington Street West in Hintonburg).

Parks for Kids

Ottawa is a city full of great parks. Here are a few good ones for kids:

St Luke's Park, Elgin at Frank Streets, behind the Second Cup: Operated by the Jack Purcell Community Centre, this is one of the cleanest and safest closed-in parks in the downtown area. Various play structures include swings, basketball nets, and a summer pool. The Bethell Field House was once a field hospital in the 1920s.

Dundonald Park, Somerset West at Bay Streets: Home of the Centretown Movies (where a screen is set up in the park for summer showings of popular films), the small play structure and sandpit are enclosed to keep the small kids in and the bigger kids out. Dundonald is also known as "beer park" in some circles, but don't let that deter you from bringing your kids here; it gets this nickname by virtue of being situated across the street from the Beer Store. Look for the plaques directly across from the store dedicated to Russian file clerk **Igor Gouzenko** (see p. 137), who lived in the apartment building across the street at 511 Somerset Street West.

Strathcona Park, Laurier Avenue East at Range Road, Sandy Hill: This park is filled with huge open spaces and various play structures. The imposing fountain at the top of the hill was presented to the City of Ottawa in 1909 by Donald Smith, a.k.a. Baron Strathcona, statesman, railway builder, and businessman, who drove the last spike in the railway that crossed the country.

Strathcona Park, Bank Street at Strathcona Avenue: Don't let the name repeated from above fool you; this is a completely separate park in the Glebe. There aren't any playgrounds here, but some lovely trees to run around under.

Andrew Haydon Park, Holly Acres Road and Carling Avenue: Located on the shores of the Ottawa River in the west end of the city, this park is named after a former mayor of the City of Nepean. It features a lovely view of Britannia Bay and includes a picnic area, artificial lake, concession stands, washrooms, and a yacht club. Swimming is *not* recommended.

Fair Thee Well

Throughout the Ottawa Valley, whether in Ontario or across the river into Quebec, you can find a county fair almost every single weekend of the summer. Here are a few of the highlights, if you feel like going for a short day trip:

The Shawville Fair: Shawville, Quebec (1 hr drive west): Started in 1856, this county fair is held on the Labour Day weekend every year (*shawvillefair.ca*).

Carp Fair: Carp (1 hr drive west): Held near the end of September every year, the Carp fair also holds an ongoing Farmer's Market (*carpfair.on.ca*).

The Glengarry Highland Games: Maxville (1 hr drive east along the 417 Hwy.): the largest Highland Games in North America, and one of the largest in the world. Founded in 1948 (with a couple of years off for World War II), the games are held from Thursday to Saturday on the August long weekend (the first weekend of the month) in Glengarry County. Events include the North American Pipe Band Championships and the highland

TATTOO YOU

Looking for an Ottawa souvenir that's perhaps more personal (and permanent) than a Parliament Buildings snowglobe? Get inked up at any of these local tattoo parlours: **The Ink Spot** (*429 Bank St., 237-1331, theinkspot.ca*), **Living Colour Tattoo** (*412 Dalhousie St., 241-4961, living-colour.com*), and **Original Universal Tattoo Studio** (*156 Rideau St., 236-3866*). Given the number of health and safety regulations they have to adhere to, tattoo parlours are always far safer (and cleaner) than you might think. And no, they won't tattoo your kid without your permission; the minimum age with parental consent is 16, and the minimum without is 18.

MORE FESTIVALS:

Capital Pride: Celebrating the LGBTQ community in both Ottawa and Gatineau every year, its highlight, of course, is the parade, which usually runs along Somerset Street West from Elgin Street heading west, before turning south on Bank Street (prideottawa.ca).

Carnival of Cultures: Held during the weekend before Canada Day, the open-air performances at the Astrolabe Theatre at Nepean Point (behind the National Gallery) showcase a variety of cultural backgrounds and experiences (carnivalofcultures.ca).

Grand Rire de Gatineau: Yes, Gatineau has its own comedy festival, highlighting some of the best Quebec and international French-language performers in both indoor and outdoor venues (grandrire.com).

Ottawa Folk Festival: Held in the middle of August in beautiful Britannia Park in the west end, this is considered one of the best music festivals in the country, and was recently named as one of the "Top 50 Ontario Festivals." They also hold a series of concerts and special performances throughout the year (ottawafolk.org).

dance competition, as well as the usual caber, sheaf, and hammer toss, and more kilts than you can shake a stick at. Glengarry is not only the oldest county in the province, but the home of the largest concentration of Scottish immigrants in Canada (glengarryhighlandgames.com).

The **Williamstown Fair**, Williamstown (1½ hr drive east): called the home of Canada's oldest annual fair, Williamstown sits in the middle of Glengarry County (williamstownfair.com).

For other Ottawa Valley fairs, and other events, check out: ottawavalley.org/ calendarofevents.html

Feeling Festive

Perhaps Ottawa should be dubbed the "City of Festivals," given the numerous events held here per season. (For all festival listings in Ottawa check out ottawafestivals.ca.) Here are just a few of them:

Winterlude

Staged over three consecutive weekends in February, the annual **Winterlude** festival consists of more than **120 indoor and outdoor activities**, which, after 20 years, attract over 1.2 million visitors to the Ottawa region annually. Events include: live music shows, professional figure skating performances, snow sculpting and ice carving competitions, the world's largest skate-a-thon, and a bed race that draws crowds from miles around. In Gatineau, **Jacques Cartier Park** is transformed into a winter wonderland, the world's largest children's snow playground. Another feature is the downhill and cross-country skiing, including the **Winterman and Winterwoman Sports Weekend**, the 21-kilometre (13-mi) run that follows "Canada's discovery route" (Confederation Boulevard). World renowned, the event

Photo: Charles Earl

also is part of the prestigious world loppett (cross-country ski race) circuit. And, of course, always a highlight of Winterlude is **skating on the Rideau Canal**, featuring a "rink" that stretches 7.8 kilometres (4.8 mi) from the Château Laurier to Dow's Lake.

Canadian Tulip Festival

Photo: Charles Earl

This event occurs every year in May, when millions of tulips blossom throughout the city. It includes several official locations and attraction sites. Toronto folk-rock band the **Skydiggers** play an annual show here, and have been named the official band of the festival. How cool is that?
567-4447 or 1-800-66-TULIP, tulipfestival.ca

A Festival Fit for a Queen

During World War II, Queen Wilhelmina of the Netherlands, along with her daughter Princess Juliana and

Photo: Charles Earl

Ottawa Fringe Festival: This annual festival in June showcases local, national, and international performers and playwrights, some with shows touring other Fringe Festivals across Canada *(ottawafringe.com)*.

Ottawa Greek Fest: Every August, spend a few weeks of living "the Greek way" *(ottawagreekfest.com)*.

Ottawa International Animation Festival: The largest event of its kind in North America, this competitive festival showcases the best of cutting-edge, trend-setting animation as well as industry standards *(ottawa.awn.com)*.

Ottawa International Busker Festival: Showcasing "five days of unorthodox entertainment," the Busker Festival has some of the best musicians, jugglers, fire-eaters, storytellers, comedians, magicians, and mimes from Canada and around the world *(sparksstreetmall.com)*.

Ottawa Lumière Festival: Ottawa's nighttime festival, celebrating "the magic and mystical beauty of light" in New Edinburgh, with dance, music, poetry, and *thousands* of lanterns *(lumiereottawa.com)* (see photo above).

PLUGGED IN
If you're going to spend any time in a strange city, one of the first things you'll probably want to find is an Internet connection. There are plenty of free venues at various community centres and public libraries around town, but obviously it's much faster if you just bite the bullet and pay for it. Here are some of the best options: **IGO Cyber House** *(open 24 hours, 223 Bank St., 567-0567)*, **Café Internet** *(288 Bank St., 230-9000)*, **Internet Zone** *(176 Rideau St., 789-3446)*, and **Jazz' OO Café** *(33 Beechwood Ave., 746-4955)*.

her children, lived at **Stornoway House** in Rockcliffe Park during the time of their exile (some considered this an act of cowardice, leaving the Dutch people to suffer Nazi wrath). During her time in Ottawa, where few people recognized her, Princess Juliana sent her two daughters to public school, did her own grocery shopping, and even went to the movies unescorted. In 1945, Princess Juliana returned to the Netherlands with her mother to set up a temporary Dutch government, becoming Queen Juliana three years later. Once home, she expressed her gratitude to Canada, specifically to the City of Ottawa and its people, by sending the city 100,000 tulip bulbs. The following year, she sent another 20,500 bulbs, with the request that a portion of these be planted at the grounds of the Ottawa Civic Hospital where she had given birth to Princess Margriet in 1943. (The Parliament of Canada passed a special law at the time temporarily declaring the delivery room Dutch soil to ensure that the Princess was born in the Netherlands.) Queen Juliana promised Ottawa an annual gift of tulips during her lifetime to show her lasting appreciation for Canada's wartime hospitality. Out of these donations, Ottawa has held its first annual Canadian Tulip Festival in May since 1953, and the 1967 festival was opened by Queen Juliana herself.

LadyFest Ottawa

Photo: Samantha Purdy, photographed by Sara Guindon

This event is (according to the website) a "non-profit, primarily women-organized music and arts festival that is open to everyone." The festival originated in Olympia, Washington, in 2000, along with other Canadian cities such as Toronto, Guelph, and Halifax; it first came to Ottawa in 2001. As well as their annual festival of music shows, craft fairs, and DIY workshops, they hold various events throughout the year. A magnificent mixture of kick-ass, no bullshit, and health-wise attitudes. Check out their website for more information *(ladyfestottawa.com)*.

Ottawa's Carnegie Library

Photo: Archives of Ontario S-2047

Library books were circulated in Ottawa as early as 1871, but the town had no building for that purpose until the early 1900s (before that, it was host to a number of reading rooms in hotel lobbies, as well as some "small fee-based libraries for working men"). In 1897, citizens formed the Public Library Board in order to persuade the city council to free funds to build a library. Eventually, Mayor William Morris wrote to American philanthropist Andrew Carnegie (who, in the end, helped fund libraries around the world) soliciting funds for the proposed library. Carnegie donated $100,000 toward the building, provided the city would donate the land and $7,500 annually for upkeep. Although more than generous, many city councillors voted against the offer, believing their part of the bargain too expensive. But public opinion prevailed; the city purchased land at the corner of Metcalf and Laurier Streets, and construction began in 1905. Carnegie arrived in May 1906 to officially open the building, which was named the Carnegie Library in honour of his generosity.

We're Not in Kansas Anymore

You shouldn't confuse our **University of Ottawa** (uottawa.ca) with **Ottawa University** in Kansas (ottawa. edu). The University of Ottawa, one of the city's main post-secondary attractions, is as old as the city itself and is home to the only fully bilingual university press in Canada. Founded in 1848 by the Oblates of Mary Immaculate, within a year it was known as the College of Bytown. By 1861 it was the University of Ottawa, and over the following decades, it became a secular institute offering parallel courses in both official languages. Still, while **Carleton University** may have the art gallery (carleton.ca/gallery), the University of Ottawa is the one with the Fine Arts program. (Does *that* make sense to anyone?) Ottawa University in Ottawa, Kansas

BOARD OUT OF YOUR MIND?

Ottawa is home to a number of **skateboard parks**, including a variety of great outdoor parks open in the summer: **Blackburn Park**, 200-202 Glen Park Drive; **Andy Shields Park**, 1448 Meadow Drive; **Orléans Recreation Complex**, 1490 Youville Drive; **Malvern Park**, 100 Malvern Drive; **Centennial Park**, 5572 Doctor Leach Drive; **Osgoode Community Centre**, 5660 Osgoode Main Street; **Splash Wave Pool and Park**, 2040 Ogilvie Road; **Stittsville Arena**, 10 Warner Colpitts Street; **Walter Baker Park**, 100 Walter Baker Place; **Centrepointe at "The Fountain,"** Woodroffe west of Baseline Road. And check out the indoor spots at **Stittsville Arena**, 10 Warner-Colpitts Street, and **McNabb Park**, 435 Bronson Avenue. They may not all be downtown, but you might have less chance of being hassled by city bylaw enforcers.

(the town was founded in the middle of Ottawa Indian territory in 1864), is almost as old as ours, and was founded by Baptist missionaries working with the Native American population as an ecumenical college in 1865. So be careful where you send in your application for admission.

CENTRE OF ACTIVITY

One of the most active community centres in the downtown core is the **Glebe Community Centre**. Originally called Abbotsford House, built in 1867 by Alexander Mutchmor, it had a few incarnations as a church before finally being sold to the City in 1974 to become the Glebe Community Centre. A centerpiece of the family-oriented neighbourhood, the main hall is a great place for kids and offers child-related events throughout the week during the day (including a small kitchen for lunches) and a series of community and craft fairs on the weekends. The entire building was closed for renovation for a year and reopened again in 2005, and you can easily get lost in the maze of stairs and little tiny rooms throughout. *175 Third Ave., 564-1058, gnag.ca*

Centres of Culture

A highlight of Chinatown (or "Somerset Heights") is the **Ottawa Chinese Community Service Centre** *(381 Kent St., 235-1032, ottawachineseservices. org)*, established in 1975 to advance the social and economic integration of people of Chinese descent into the mainstream society in Ottawa. The facility assists with settlement, counselling, language training, and community development. Although if you need its services because you can't speak English, odds are you probably aren't picking up this book.

Other community centres in Ottawa providing similar services for other communities across the region include the **Italian Canadian Community Centre of the National Capital Region** *(101–865 Gladstone*

Ave., 567-4532, ncf.ca/ita), the **Soloway Jewish Community Centre** (21 Nadolny Sachs Private, 798-9818, jccottawa.com), the **Ottawa Hungarian Community Centre** (43 Capital Dr., Nepean, 225-8754, ottawamagyarhaz.org), and the **Somali Centre for Family Services** (1719 Bank St., 526-2075, somalifamilyservices.org). Not exactly a community centre, but along the same lines, there's always the **Irish Society of the National Capital Region** (irishsocietyncr.com), providing information on scholarships, genealogy, and various cultural events, including its annual Irish Week in March, when it hosts of the St Patrick's Day parade.

Resting Places

The most famous eternal resting place in Ottawa is **Beechwood Cemetery** (280 Beechwood Ave., 741-9530, beechwoodcemetery.com). Established in 1873 as a Protestant counterpart to nearby Notre Dame cemetery, Beechwood is a National Historic Site, and only one of four cemeteries in the country to be designated as such. Have a look at the sections where veterans from the Northwest Rebellion (1885), World War II, and recent United Nations campaigns rest in peace. Also interred here are our eighth prime minister (and the handsome fellow on our $100 bill), **Sir Robert Borden** (1854–1937); the father of Canada's Medicare system, **Tommy Douglas** (1904–1986); the inventor of standard time, **Sir Sandford Fleming** (1827–1915); Ottawa lumber baron **J. R. Booth** (1827–1925); the Saskatchewan poet **John Newlove** (1938–2003); and Confederation poet Archibald Lampman (1861–1899). Lampman even wrote a poem that suits this place:

> Here the dead sleep – the
> quiet dead. No sound dis-
> turbs them ever, and no storm
> dismays.

Meanwhile, **Pinecrest Cemetery** (2500 Baseline Rd., 829-3600) is a veritable hockey hall of fame. Some notable skaters spending their eternal off-season here include: Boston Bruins' left winger **Arthur Gordon Bruce** (1919–1997), former Bruins and Ottawa Senators players **Harry Alexander Connor** (1904–1947), **Cyril Joseph "Cy" Denneny** (1891–1970) – one of the

A HIDDEN RETREAT

Even though it earned an award for excellence for the developers who created it in 1980, the **Fifth Avenue Court** at Bank Street and Fifth Avenue is almost completely empty most of the time. It's a quiet place with indoor patios for the businesses that surround the fountain and courtyard, including the British-style pub, the **Arrow & the Loon**. They've been known to host the National Arts Centre Orchestra in their courtyard from time to time.

DIALED IN

At the corner of Sussex Drive and Bruyère Street, on the Mother House of the Grey Nuns of the Cross (the current **Elizabeth Bruyère Health Centre**), check out the sundials just overhead. Erected in 1851 (at just about the second-storey line at the corner), the vertical sundials were designed by Père Allard, geometry teacher to the nuns.

GOING ON FAITH

To connect with the Buddhist community in Ottawa, look into any of these organizations: the **Ottawa Buddhist Society** (ottawabuddhistsociety.com), the **Ottawa Shambhala Meditation Centre** (984 Wellington St. W., 725-9321, shambhalaottawa.ca), or the **Buddhism in the National Capital of Canada** website (dharma.ncf.ca). The **Joyful Land Buddhist Centre in Chinatown** (879 Somerset St. W., 234-4347, meditateinottawa.com) has its own bookstore, located at the back. For the Muslim community, there is a particularly attractive building in the Parkdale area known as the **Ottawa Mosque** (251 Northwestern Ave., 722-8763, omaonline.ca). If you drive a motorcycle, there's the **Capital City Bikers' Church** at Arlington Woods Free Methodist Church (225 McClellan Rd., Nepean, bikerschurch.com). Founded in 2002, it promotes itself as having "a desire to share the message of God's unconditional love and His amazing grace with the motorcycle community of the National Capital Region." For other churches in the Ottawa area (of various denominations), you can always check out ottawachurches.ncf.ca.

Photo: Charles Earl

top-scoring left wings of his era (when he retired, he was the top goal getter in the history of the Ottawa Senators) – and Senators' players **Erskine Rockcliffe Ronan** (1889–1937), **Gerald Edmund Shannon** (1910–1983), **Allan "Big Pete" Shields** (1906–1975) (who won the Stanley Cup with the Montreal Maroons in 1934-5), and **Alexander "Boots" Smith** (1902–1963).

The most prominent Catholic cemetery in the city is **Notre Dame Cemetery** (455 Montreal Rd.), the final resting place of hockey greats **Alex Connell** (1902–1958), **Tommy Smith** (1885–1966), and **Aurel Joliat** (1901–1986), as well as photographer **Yousuf Karsh** (1908–2002), World War I hero (awarded the Victoria Cross) **Filip Konowal** (1886–1959), statesman **Louis-Félix Pinault** (1852–1906), and Prime Minister **Sir Wilfred Laurier** (1841–1919), along with his wife Zoé.

further reading

City on the Ottawa (Minister of Public Works, 1961)

The Ontario Book of Days, by Robbins Elliott (Dundurn Press, 1988)

Ottawa, by James Hale and Joanne Milner (Macfarlane, Walter & Ross, 1996)

Ottawa, City of the Big Ears: The Intimate, Living Story of a City and a Capital, by Robert Haig (Haig, 1969)

Ottawa: Making a Capital, edited by Jeff Keshen (University of Ottawa Press, 2001)

Ottawa Stories: Images through the Seasons, by Paul von Baich, with F. J. McEvoy and Mary Ann Simpkins (Bubna-Lennkh Publishing, 1994)

Ottawa: The Capital of Canada, by Shirley E. Woods, Jr (Doubleday, 1980)

Ottawa with Kids: The Complete Family Travel Guide to Attractions, Sites and Events in Ottawa, by James Hale and Joanne Milner (Macfarlane, Walter & Ross, 1996)

Secret Ottawa: The Unique Guidebook to Ottawa's Hidden Sites, Sounds, & Tastes, by Laura Byrne Paquet (ECW Press, 2000)

index

index

index

index

index

index

index

index

Photo: Christina Riley

rob mclennan is an Ottawa-born & based writer, publisher, critic, and artist, and the author of numerous books and chapbooks of poetry, fiction, and nonfiction, including the poetry collection *The Ottawa City Project* and the novel *White*. He has also edited over a dozen anthologies of poetry, fiction, and critical writing, and is very active in Ottawa's literary scene.